HOME BAKES

CAROLIÉ DE KOSTER

PHOTOGRAPHY BY VOLKER MIROS

LANNICE SNYMAN INC.

CONTENTS

First Published 2001 by
Lannice Snyman Inc.
PO Box 26344, Hout Bay 7872,
South Africa
E-mail lannice@iafrica.com

Author Carolié de Koster
Publisher & editor Lannice Snyman
Photographer Volker Miros SASC
Food stylist Tamsin Snyman
Photo-shoot assistant Angela Miros
Designer Heather Dittmar
Copy editor Brenda Brickman
Proofreader Elizé Lubbe
Colour separation UCA Repro

Printed and bound in Singapore by
Tien Wah Press (Pte) Limited

Eyelike MF digital camera by Jenoptik
Photographic props kindly loaned by
Clay Café, Hout Bay
The Yellow Door, Gardens
Mystique Glassware & Gifts, Sea Point

ISBN 0 620 27616 9

INTRODUCTION

Home baking immediately conjures up images of breads, fresh from the oven, home-made sausage rolls and toasty warm muffins, and baking – with your own two hands – a classic cake that looks and tastes as good as the coffee-shop version. *Home Bakes* will teach you what it takes to make baking easy and successful – and most of all, fun. For some, baking comes so naturally it's almost second nature; for others it seems mysteriously daunting. For most of us, it is somewhere in between.

There are, however, always prerequisites to successful baking. First on the list is a good recipe book with reliable recipes and clear instructions. *Home Bakes* is just such a book! Having the basic baking equipment at your fingertips is also essential. Some recipes, for example, one for bread, need little in this way, while fancy, decorated cakes require specific items to ensure a perfectly turned out cake. Most important is that the correct methods of measuring, mixing and baking each recipe are followed carefully.

Home Bakes aims to meet the different needs of young and old, the experienced and the novice baker. An information section covers basic baking utensils – what they are and their functions, offers general tips that relate to many of the recipes in the book, and clarifies certain baking terms and techniques. Please read this chapter, and refer to it if ever you're in any doubt.

Successful baking is greatly influenced by the quality and freshness of the raw products used, and no amount of baking skill can disguise inferior ingredients. Flour is the cornerstone of all baking, so make sure that you purchase the best quality flour from reputable stores. Here I would like to thank the producers of Golden Cloud flours for backing this project, and for supplying me with their wonderful products to create these recipes.

I trust that this book will enable all bakers – those who bake professionally as well as those who bake simply for pleasure – to stand back and observe their efforts with pride and satisfaction. And may the cherry on the cake be the compliments or orders that will come rolling in!

Carolié de Koster

ABOUT THE AUTHOR

Carolié de Koster's food business is aptly named Foodlink, because everything that she does is professionally linked with food. After training as a dietician, she decided that practical food preparation interested her more than clinical work, so she began giving cookery courses, and now offers courses for caterers, housewives, kitchen personnel, house-keepers – in fact everyone who wishes to improve their cookery skills, whether it be for enjoyment or on a professional basis. Although she covers all aspects of cooking, baking has always been a favourite. Her cookery school is at her modern demonstration kitchen in Beaulieu, Midrand.

Carolié also travels frequently to many parts of South Africa and Namibia, lecturing to groups, gourmet clubs and hotel schools.

Working with food on a wider level led to planning of menus and kitchens and assisting with staff training for small restaurants, coffee shops, lodges and guesthouses. Training also includes presenting specific topics to students at colleges and hotel schools as well as at secondary school level.

Carolié is the author of *Rising to Perfection* (1985) and *Art of Cooking* (1998), and co-author of *Your own Guesthouse* (1999).

THE STORY OF WHEAT

An ear of wheat is the symbol of wholesomeness. A wheat field portrays a fertile land. Wheat was first cultivated by Stone Age men in the 'fertile crescent' – the land curving from the western part of present-day Iran through Iraq and Syria to the Valley of the Nile. These primitive farmers made the first crude flatbreads, probably by cooking porridge-like substances of coarsely ground grain on top of large, flat stones, heated on open fires.

During the Bronze Age, 5 000 years ago, ovens were contrived by inverting pots over heated stones to trap rising heat. This meant that larger, thicker breads could be baked. Shortly afterwards, or perhaps simultaneously, came the discovery of yeast fermentation: early cooks found that an uncooked grain of porridge, left in the open for a few hours, developed bubbles and gave off a sour smell. The thin mixture proved to be a tangy intoxicating drink – beer. The thicker mixture, when cooked after fermentation, produced a bread that was lighter and more palatable than the flatbread made with fresh dough.

Egyptians left detailed pictorial records of their sophisticated baking techniques of some 50 wheat-based breads of different shapes and flavours, for instance augmented with poppy or sesame seeds, sweetened with honey, and enriched with eggs and milk. Aside from experimenting with a variety of ingredients, they designed thick clay ovens with two levels

– one below for the fire, and an upper level for baking. The Greeks soon followed suit, however their loaves were less elaborate.

The Romans perfected the first large-scale mills. These mills – examples of which were found in the ruins of Pompeii – consisted of two large stones shaped like shallow cones. The method was simple but effective. Grain was placed between the two stones; one 'cone' was stationary, and the other was turned by a team of slaves or mules, grinding the grain to a fine powder. The 'flour' was then sifted through woven baskets to further refine it.

The Romans also invented a machine that made dough. An ox or slave walked around a large stone bowl, turning wooden paddles that mixed and kneaded the dough. Eventually specialist milling and baking techniques perfected by the Romans, were used throughout Europe. Until the 19th century, village bakers used large, tunnel-shaped brick ovens, and made the fire directly on the floor. Ovens were used communally, for few homes had ovens, and professional bakers would charge a small fee for baking home-prepared loaves.

However, even after sifting small particles of bran and pale yellow germ remained in the flour. In the 1830s Swiss millers invented the roller mill, which refined the grain to produce pure, white flour. The process is still used today. Wheat grains are first cleaned, then

passed through a series of high-speed rollers. The first rolling cracks open the grains, causing the endosperm to separate from the bran and the germ. Progressive rolling results in a white flour that is virtually pure endosperm, and passing the flour through fine sieves makes it even purer.

A wheat kernel consists of a bran coating, starchy endosperm and, inside, nutrient-rich wheat germ. For variety in texture and flavour, use both wholewheat and refined flours in baking. Wholewheat flour is rich in bran and dietary fibre, and can supplement a diet deficient in B vitamins – the vitamin essential to the body's efficient use of carbohydrates for energy. However, there is little extra nutrition in brown flour, and if you have a well-balanced diet regime, where B vitamins are supplied by other foods (such as red meat), and roughage is obtained from cereals, vegetables and fruit, it will make little dietary difference if you choose unrefined flour over refined flour.

Over the centuries baking with wheat flour has become a fine art. The unfortunate few who are allergic to wheat know how difficult it is to replace it with flour made from other grains. Wheat is the only grain that contains gluten. Gluten is a form of protein, and it plays an important role in baking, as, when moistened, beating or kneading develops the gluten, giving body to batter or dough. If a fine, crumbly texture is required, gluten development should be suppressed, and beating or kneading should be kept to a minimum.

Indonesian Spice & Chocolate Chip-Cake page 54

Gourmet Fruit Loaf page 52

A WORD FROM THE SPONSOR

Golden Cloud® wheat products are milled and marketed by Tiger Milling. These products – from the finest, whitest cake flour, to coarse and crunchy wholewheat flour – have been successfully tried and tested in the preparation of all the recipes in *Home Bakes*.

The brand name, Golden Cloud®, dates back almost a hundred years. An old photograph of the Kaffrarian Steam Mill in East London, taken in 1904, hangs on the wall in the office at the Randfontein Mill.

And the praises of Golden Cloud flours have been sung by authors of South African cookbooks since the early days of publishing. Jeanette C van Duyn's *The Household Science Cookery Book* (1920), and *Afrikaanse Kookboek* (1923) have Golden Cloud printed at the bottom of each page, and the author explains at length as to why it is better than any other. And the 6th edition of Mrs Slade's *South African Cookery Book* also contains Golden Cloud advertisement.

Golden Cloud products are found on supermarket shelves country-wide. When baking with wheat products, make sure that your pack of flour is fresh. Select pack sizes that are appropriate to the amount of flour you use in your kitchen, so that flour products do not stand in the cupboard for too long. Always store flour in clean, airtight containers.

GOLDEN CLOUD CAKE FLOUR

Pack sizes: 500 g, 1 kg, 2.5 kg, 5 kg, 10 kg and 12.5 kg

This versatile cake flour is refined enough for the most delicate of cakes, and is strong enough for baking light-textured breads, rolls and buns.

GOLDEN CLOUD SELF-RAISING FLOUR

Pack sizes: 500 g, 1 kg, 2.5 kg

Extremely convenient to use, as the correct amount of rising agent – which is completely tasteless – has been blended with the flour, ruling out the need for additional rising agents. Self-raising flour is perfect for quick bakes such as scones, crumpets and rusks.

GOLDEN CLOUD WHITE BREAD FLOUR

Pack sizes: 1 kg, 2.5 kg, 5 kg, 10 kg, 12.5 kg

This flour is not as white nor as light as cake flour, but is excellent for breads and other bakes that have a slightly more chewy, firm texture. Increase the kneading time of bread flour dough to make the dough smooth and elastic. The flavour and colour of bread-flour products will be slightly different to those made with cake flour.

GOLDEN CLOUD BROWN BREAD FLOUR

Pack sizes: 1 kg, 2.5 kg, 5 kg, 10 kg, 12.5 kg

Wheaten bran added to white bread flour results in brown bread flour, which is fabulous for making light brown bread and rolls. Brown bread flour is often combined with other flours in recipes that call for a coarser texture and lighter colour.

GOLDEN CLOUD KRAKLEY WHEAT WHOLEWHEAT FLOUR

Pack sizes: 1 kg, 2,5 kg

Crushed wheat is added to flour to make it coarser and darker in colour. Products made with Krakley Wheat are wonderfully crunchy and grainy. Take care when making rusks, though, as the crushed wheat bits can become very hard after drying out. Use only a small amount of Krakley Wheat, or use brown bread flour instead.

GOLDEN CLOUD SEMOLINA

Pack sizes: 500 g, 1 kg

Fine, granular semolina adds a nutty flavour and crisp texture to baked products ranging from biscuits to breads. It's also used as a thickening agent for pie fillings.

ACE SUPER MAIZE MEAL

Pack sizes: 1 kg, 2.5 kg

Maize products packed by Tiger Milling are also included in recipes in *Home Bakes*.

BAKING TECHNIQUES & METHODS

The cornerstone of good baking is a reliable and successful recipe. The recipe should, in order to prevent inaccurate measuring, clearly and neatly specify the ingredients. The method should be written in an easy-to-follow, step-by-step sequence, but may include certain baking terminologies that can be misinterpreted. It is to this end that I have included a list of baking terms and their definitions, utensils and their uses, and the breakdown of some basic ingredients in this book.

Before starting to bake, carefully read through the recipe. Make sure that ingredients and utensils required are on hand, and methods are understood.

BAKING TERMS

Beat: An action whereby you mix ingredients and combine them evenly, simultaneously introducing air into the mixture to make it light and fluffy. Beating can be done by hand, using a spoon, fork, wire whisk, or manual beaters (egg beaters; rotary beaters). An electric hand beater and large electric mixer is ideal if you bake often or on a large scale. When beating egg whites with an electric mixer, fit the balloon whisk.

Blend: An action whereby you combine ingredients to such a degree that you achieve a uniform texture. Blending can be done with a spoon, by hand or with an electric beater, or in a food processor or liquidiser.

Bake blind: When a pie crust is baked without the filling. Line the pie plate with pastry and cover with light foil, extending it well over the sides, and pressing it down onto the pastry and into the corners. This ensures that the pie shell will retain its shape during baking. Bake the pastry, covered, for 20 minutes at 200°C. Carefully remove the foil, and continue baking until the pastry is light golden brown. This method is superior to the outdated way of baking with waxed paper filled with dried beans or rice which don't support the sides of the crust.

Fold in: Combining ingredients lightly yet thoroughly with a whisk, spatula or metal spoon without stirring vigorously.

Grease: Hard margarine is recommended for greasing cake tins, baking trays and ovenproof dishes. The nonstick quality is good while the taste is neutral. Butter and oil may be used, but butter tends to make products stick, and browns more quickly than margarine, and oil imparts a specific flavour which becomes more pronounced if baked products are stored for a few days. Grease generously but evenly and, in the case of muffin cups, grease on top of the muffin tin as well to prevent the muffin caps from breaking away from the bases. It may sometimes be necessary to line the tin/s with baking paper before greasing, but sprinkling with flour is not much use.

Sift: It's no longer considered necessary to sift flour to remove foreign particles. Fresh flour is clean and pure, and simply needs to be aerated by turning it out into a large flour container, or scooping and sprinkling it back with the measuring jug or cup before measuring out. There are only two reasons to sift flour; to combine it evenly with lumpy ingredient such as cornflour or cocoa, or to add air to cakes that rely solely on air expansion to rise during baking.

Measuring dry ingredients: Fill the scoop or cup in a relaxed way without shaking it into the cup, and scrape off the surplus with the back of a knife. In most cases the dry ingredients, including spices, baking powder, salt and sugar can be stirred together in the mixing bowl to combine evenly.

UTENSILS

BAKING PAPER: Nonstick baking paper is useful as it doesn't need greasing and won't stick to food. Don't grease it, as this reduces the nonstick quality. Waxed paper, also known as greaseproof paper, is transparent and coated with wax to prevent moisture loss and to keep food fresh. Use it to line baking tins, well greased to prevent sticking.

BAKING TINS: These should correspond as far as possible with the specifications in each recipe, and should be large enough to allow for expansion during baking, yet small enough to support the product. Good quality rustproof aluminium tins are the best choice. If metal tins have been treated with a nonstick coating, or have a dark colour, it may be necessary to reduce the oven temperature slightly, as they reflect less heat than aluminium tins and result in very dark crusts. To measure baking tins or dishes, take the inside measurements on the top of the container.

BAKING TRAYS/RECTANGULAR OVENPROOF DISHES: Small baking trays are 30 x 2 cm; medium trays 38 x 28 cm. In most cases the depth of the baking tray is 3 cm, while dishes range between 3 cm (shallow rectangular dishes) and 6 cm (deep rectangular dishes). Before using glassware in the oven, be sure that it's ovenproof, and have a mark of identification.

BEATERS/MIXERS: Whisks, hand beaters, electric beaters, electric mixers and food processors simplify mixing and kneading. Wire whisks like flat or balloon whisks are available in different sizes for different volumes, and ensure that batters and fillings are lump-free. Whisks are also useful for lighter beating and folding in.

CAKE TINS:

ROUND CAKE TINS: These are measured by diameter, and should preferably be springform or loose-bottomed. Solid tins should be lined with baking paper to facilitate the removal of the cake. The depth of an average tin is 6 cm.

TUBE PANS (FLUTED/DEEP-RING TINS): An assortment of tube tins is available, but the tins used in this book are mainly fluted Bundt or Kugelhopf tins (for plain or simply glazed cakes), or the straight-sided Angel Cake Tin (for plain cakes or those that will be filled and iced). Angel Cake Tins, or deep-ring tins allow hot air to circulate through the centre while baking, ensuring even cooking right through.

Large, loose-based tubular aluminium pans (about 25 x 11 cm) have a smooth base, straight sides and perfectly sealed base to prevent leaking. The tin has three little 'legs' that allow air to circulate while cooling the cake in the inverted tin. A nonstick coating is not suitable, as the inverted cake should cling to the ungreased tin while cooling, without falling out, to ensure a feather-light texture.

LOAF TINS: The length of an average large loaf tin is 28 cm; the volume is 2.25 litres. The length of an average medium loaf tin is 26 cm; the volume is 1.75 litres. The length of an average small loaf tin is 23 cm; the volume is 1 litre.

Tin shapes vary significantly, some are longer and narrower, and others shorter and wider, but still have approximately the same volume. To determine your own tin size, fill with water and compare the volume with the volume measurements given for the small, medium and large loaf tins in this book.

INGREDIENTS

All of the ingredients called for in *Home Bakes* are readily available from any well-stocked supermarket. Ingredients should be fresh, which isn't a problem now that most items are date-stamped.

Butter and hard margarine
Butter or hard margarine plays an important role in baking. Butter is a pure form of saturated animal fat, while margarine is a man-made alternative which comprises polyunsaturated vegetable oils. Results achieved in baking are similar, especially when the recipe includes well-flavoured ingredients such as spices or cocoa. In subtly flavoured cakes and biscuits, though, the flavour of butter, or lack of it, will be noticeable. Only use hard butter or margarine bricks; spreadable (tub) margarines and butters are unsuitable for baking.

MEASURING, WEIGHING AND MELTING BUTTER AND HARD MARGARINE.
Use a scale or use the water replacement method: pour enough water to cover the butter or margarine into a transparent, clearly graded measuring jug. Add butter or margarine and press it under the water until it rises sufficiently to the replace the measure of butter or margarine required. For example, pour 250 ml water into a jug. To measure 100 ml butter or margarine, add it to the water, and press it below the water level to raise the level to 350 ml.

Melted butter or margarine is measured in millilitres. Melt in a saucepan over low heat, or in a bowl or jug in the microwave on Medium. Before beating, creaming or blending butter or hard margarine, remove it from the fridge and let it stand at room temperature for at least 30 minutes in summer, longer in winter. If time is limited, microwave butter on Defrost for about 20 seconds to soften without melting.

Chocolate
Always use good quality chocolate slabs. Chocolate chips are readily available to use

MEASURING UTENSILS:

SCOOPS OR JUGS: These items are available in the following standard sizes: 50 ml, 100 ml, 125 ml, 200 ml, 250 ml, 500 ml. Transparent heat-resistant measuring jugs are sized as 250 ml, 500 ml, 1 litre, and 2.5 litres.

MEASURING SPOONS: These items are available in the following standard sizes: 1 ml, 2 ml, 5 ml, 10 ml, 15 ml, and 25/30 ml.

MIXING BOWLS: These items are available in different sizes, and in plastics or glass.

OVEN: Oven temperature should always be as stated in the recipe, and the heat level must be maintained while baking.

If you suspect that your oven doesn't function well, have it serviced. If it tends to bake too hot from below or from the top, shield cover the oven rack with heavy foil.

PIE PLATES/DISHES: Purchase only ovenproof pie plates/dishes, and preferably those that have slightly slanted sides to make serving easier. Pie plates should be at least 3 cm and no more than 5 cm deep.

PIPING BAG: Fitted with different shaped and sized nozzles, piping bags are used to pipe rosettes or decorative strips of cream, icing, custard or fillings onto cakes.

Purchase a strong and durable bag, that won't tear under pressure, when piping firm mixtures such as choux pastry, and can withstand a soaking in a diluted bleaching agent, and scrubbing to keep it hygienically clean.

SCALES: Good quality small (up to 500 g) and large (up to 2 kg) scales are indispensable for efficient weighing of ingredients.

SIEVES: These are needed to refine lumpy dry ingredients, such as cocoa powder and icing sugar.

SPATULAS: Spatulas made of plastic are firm yet flexible, and are essential for scraping batter from bowls.

in biscuits and cakes, and to use as a garnish. Or use chocolate vermicelli instead. Large irregular-shaped chocolate chips don't disperse evenly in batter, and tend to sink. If preferred, chop the required amount of chocolate by hand or in a food processor.

MELTING CHOCOLATE IN THE MICROWAVE OVEN

Break dark, milk or cooking chocolate into a suitable bowl, cover and microwave on Medium for 1–2 minutes until softened: test with the tip of a teaspoon. Stir gently until smooth and use as required. White chocolate doesn't melt successfully in the microwave without caramelizing, and should only be melted over the steam of simmering water.

MELTING CHOCOLATE OVER STEAM

Break the chocolate into a heat-resistant bowl or the top of a double-boiler and melt over the steam of simmering water. Don't allow the bowl to touch the water. Cover and leave for about 5 minutes until soft. Stir gently until smooth and use as required.

Chocolate leaves

Select nonpoisonous leaves with pronounced veins (make sure they haven't been sprayed with insecticide), and wash and dry well. Brush melted chocolate evenly and fairly thickly onto the underside only of the leaves. Wipe the chocolate from the edges of the leaves and place onto a small tray. Refrigerate until hard. Carefully pull away and discard the fresh leaves, and store chocolate leaves in an airtight container in a cool place or the fridge.

Chocolate shavings

Hold the chocolate bar upright and make thin shavings with a swivel-bladed vegetable peeler or sharp, smooth-edged knife. Refrigerate in an airtight container until required.

Chocolate curls

Pour melted chocolate onto a granite slab, metal baking tray or glass counter-saver. Spread evenly, about 10 mm thick, and leave

just to the point of setting, but not yet hard. Scrape chocolate into curls with a sharp, smooth-edged knife or wallpaper scraper held at an angle. Refrigerate in an airtight container.

Cinnamon sugar

Cinnamon mixed with sugar, is perfect for sprinkling over baked goodies. Mix 125 ml sugar with 10 ml ground cinnamon. Store in a small bottle in the cupboard.

Cornflour

Cornflour is made from the white heart of maize kernels, ground to a fine, silky powder. It's used mainly as a thickening agent. When used to partly replace cake flour, the texture of baked products and custards is more delicate.

Eggs

Eggs used in this book are free-range, where possible, extra-large, and weigh 60 g in the shell. If larger eggs are used, the raw mixture will appear thinner, but will thicken more during cooking.

The opposite applies when smaller eggs are used, as the volume of the cake will be slightly more or slightly less.

If using smaller eggs, add an extra egg for every 3 eggs used. If jumbo eggs are used, use 4 eggs instead of 5, but only if more than 4 eggs are called for in the recipe.

Always store eggs in the fridge.

Flavouring agents

Flavouring agents such as vanilla essence, almond essence, cocoa, spices and herbs are all sold under the names specified in the recipes. Purchase flavouring agents in realistic quantities to prevent them from becoming stale and diminishing in flavour. Store in sealed containers in a cool, dark place.

Gelatine

Gelatine has a limited shelf life, so purchase only enough to last for about 3 months, and store in an airtight container in a cool, dry place. To dissolve gelatine, pour the specified liquid into a jug or cup and sprinkle gelatine on top. Allow to 'sponge' for a minute, then dissolve by standing the jug or cup in a container of hot water, or microwave on Medium for the time suggested.

Take care not to overheat, because gelatine boils over easily and the setting ability will be impaired.

Always mix gelatine very thoroughly into the base, making sure to cool it first, or stir in a little of the cool ingredients before adding it to the base, otherwise it will set in strings or lumps.

Nuts

Nuts – specifically almonds, brazils, cashews, hazelnuts, macadamias, mixed nuts, peanuts, pecans, pistachios and walnuts – are frequently used in baking.

Fresh nuts last well for up to 3 months in sealed containers in a cool cupboard, and much longer if frozen.

ROASTING NUTS

Nuts are far more aromatic and flavourful if cooked in their natural oils.

Spread nuts in a single layer onto a baking tray and bake in a moderate oven at about 160°C until light golden. Stir once or twice, and watch closely; when the oil becomes hot, the nuts tend to scorch easily and become dark and bitter. Allow to cool and store in an airtight container.

To roast hazelnuts, preheat the oven to 180°C and spread the nuts onto a baking tray. Bake for about 10 minutes until the skins crack and the nuts are lightly roasted. Don't allow them to become to dark, because they'll become bitter and lose their sweet, fragrant aroma. Allow to cool, then rub between your palms to remove most of the skins.

CHOPPING NUTS

Place no more than 100 g at a time into a food processor and chop, using the pulse action to prevent overprocessing. Or grind coarsely in a nut grinder. Take care you don't end up with an oily paste.

Red sprinkle mix

This versatile mixed spice powder, perfect for sprinkling onto any savoury foods, is called for in many recipes in this book. Combine two-thirds paprika with one-third cayenne pepper in a spice bottle with a sprinkle top, and mix well. Paprika adds colour and cayenne pepper adds flavour.

Yeast

Instant dry yeast is the quickest, easiest yeast to use in baking. It must not be dissolved in water beforehand; simply add it to the dry ingredients before adding the liquid. Instant dry yeast comes in 10 g (15 ml) sachets. Store in a cool, dry place.

Watch the 'use by' date of the packet; an unopened packet has a shelf life of 12 months. Once the packet is open, use on the same day. The steps for yeast dough with instant yeast are as follows:

1 Mix instant yeast with some of the flour (if yeast becomes wet before it's mixed with flour it will absorb liquid, leaving grey spots in the dough). Add the remaining ingredients (not the extra flour) and mix well. Watchpoint: the liquid should be lukewarm (body temperature).

2 Add just enough extra flour to obtain a soft dough. If it's too stiff it will be difficult to knead, take longer to rise, and yield a dry end product that won't last well. Turn dough out onto a floured surface and knead until smooth and elastic. To mix and knead in an electric mixer, use the dough hook and cover the bowl with a splashguard, lid or cloth. Make the dough quite soft to ensure that the mixer will be able to knead comfortably. Place the mixer far from the edge of the work surface; if it moves while kneading it may fall off. Knead for about two-thirds of the time recommended for hand kneading, and finish by hand, adding additional flour to achieve the desired consistency.

3 Return the dough to the bowl, cover and allow to rise in a protected, warm spot, at room temperature, until doubled in bulk. In cold weather, warm the dough slightly by placing the covered bowl in the sun or in a switched-off, slightly warmed oven. Dough rises well if the bowl is placed in a second bowl of warm water. To speed up rising, either use more yeast or increase the temperature slightly. Don't make the dough too warm.

4 Punch down and shape as explained in each recipe. Allow to rise, uncovered, until doubled again, and bake as explained in the recipe.

MEASUREMENTS & CONVERSION TABLES

VOLUME

½ ml	⅛ teaspoon/pinch
1 ml	¼ teaspoon
2 ml	½ teaspoon
4 ml	¾ teaspoon
5 ml	1 teaspoon
10 ml	2 teaspoons
15 ml	1 tablespoon/3 teaspoons
45 ml	3 tablespoons
30 ml	⅛ cup/2 tablespoons
50 ml	⅕ cup
60 ml	¼ cup
85 ml	⅓ cup
125 ml	½ cup
175 ml	⅔ cup
200 ml	¾ cup
250 ml	1 cup
300 ml	1¼ cups
375 ml	1½ cups
500 ml	2 cups
750 ml	3 cups
1 litre	4 cups

LIQUID CONVERSIONS

METRIC	US	IMPERIAL
15 ml	1 tablespoon	½ fl oz
30 ml	⅛ cup	1 fl oz
60 ml	¼ cup	2 fl oz
125 ml	½ cup	4 fl oz
150 ml	⅔ cup	5 fl oz/¼ pint/1 gill
175 ml	¾ cup	6 fl oz
250 ml	1 cup	8 fl oz
300 ml	1¼ cups	½ pint
375 ml	1½ cups	12 fl oz
450 ml		¾ pint
500 ml	2 cups	16 fl oz
600 ml		20 fl oz/1 pint
900 ml		1½ pints
1.25 litres	5 cups	2 pints
1.9 litres		3 pints
2.5 litres	10 cups	4 pints

SOLID WEIGHT CONVERSION

15 g	½ oz
30 g	1 oz
50 g	1½ oz
60 g	2 oz
90 g	3 oz
100 g	3½ oz
125 g	4 oz/¼ pound
150 g	5 oz
175 g	6 oz
200 g	7 oz
250 g	8 oz/½ pound
270 g	9 oz
300 g	10 oz
500 g/0,5 kg	16 oz/1 lb
900 g	2 lb
1 kg	32 oz/2.2 lb

PAN SIZES

Sizes below are for round cake tins. To convert square or rectangular cake tins or baking trays from inches to millimeters, multiply by 2.5; to convert from millimeters to inches, divide by 2.5.

12.5 cm	5 inches
15 cm	6 inches
18 cm	7 inches
20 cm	8 inches
23 cm	9 inches
25 cm	10 inches
28 cm	11 inches
30 cm	12 inches

OVEN TEMPERATURES

CENTIGRADE	FAHRENHEIT	BRITISH GAS MARK
100°C	200°F	gas mark ¼
110°C	225°F	gas mark ¼
120°C	250°F	gas mark ½
130°C	260°F	gas mark ½
140°C	275°F	gas mark 1
150°C	300°F	gas mark 2
160°C	325°F	gas mark 3
170°C	340°F	gas mark 4
180°C	350°F	gas mark 4
190°C	375°F	gas mark 5
200°C	400°F	gas mark 5
220°C	425°F	gas mark 7
230°C	450°F	gas mark 8
240°C	475°F	gas mark 9
260°C	500°F	

BISCUITS & RUSKS

A cookie jar filled with home-baked biscuits appeals to all ages – from two to a hundred and two! It's the first thing we teach our children to make, because biscuits are the most forgiving of bakes and because they are so easy to mix, shape and cook. And biscuits are the first thing that cooks think about when the urge to bake strikes. Stored in airtight containers, biscuits last for weeks, depending, of course, on how well you hide them!

Rusks are uniquely South African: dunked into early morning coffee, packed into a school lunch, or munched with a warm bedtime drink. Many households have their own favourite recipes, ranging from pale, feather-light delights to coarse, tummy-filling treats. Rusks are generally more filling than biscuits, and lower in kilojoules.

The preparation procedure of all rusks is similar: dough is mixed and baked, then broken or cut into portions and dried in a low oven until crisp as can be. The oven door should be left slightly open to allow moisture to escape. A spoon can be used to keep the oven door open. The drying temperature should be low enough to dry rusks out in 6–8 hours without browning them at all. Experiment with temperatures around 60°C; some ovens will need a lower and some a higher temperature.

Biscuit and rusk recipes in this chapter come from kitchens all over the world, but many originated in South Africa, and have been passed down from one generation to the next. All of them are equally as enjoyable as ever. All keep perfectly in an airtight container.

Coconut and Oat Bars page 17

Energy Bars page 16

Soetkoekies page 18

Gourmet Choc-nut Tartlets page 22

OATMEAL SEED BISCUITS

Makes about 36 average or 24 large biscuits

These fibre-rich biscuits, with bags of protein in the form of milk powder, are perfect as a pick-me-up at any time of the day.

125 g (150 ml) butter or hard
    margarine, softened
80 g (100 ml) white sugar
80 g (100 ml) brown sugar
1 egg
2 ml vanilla essence
100 g (200 ml) Golden Cloud cake flour
30 g (75 ml) milk powder (any variety)
2 ml bicarbonate of soda
1 ml salt
135 g (375 ml) quick-cooking oats
50 g (100 ml) sunflower seeds, roasted
    in a dry frying pan

1 Preheat the oven to 180°C. Grease two medium baking trays.
2 Beat together the butter or margarine and sugars until creamy in a food processor or with an electric mixer. Add the egg and vanilla essence, and beat in. Add the flour, milk powder, bicarb, salt, oats and sunflower seeds, and mix until well blended.
3 Place heaped teaspoonfuls (for average biscuits) or tablespoonfuls (for larger biscuits) onto the baking trays, spacing them out well. Flatten slightly to make neat rounds. Bake for about 10 minutes (average biscuits) or 15 minutes (larger biscuits) until golden.
4 Transfer the biscuits to a wire rack and allow to cool. Store in an airtight container.

> ## COOK'S NOTE
> Sunflower seeds can be replaced with a mixture of seeds, or coarsely chopped nuts.

> ## COOK'S NOTES
> • To make the energy bars even more tempting, dip them into melted milk or white chocolate before wrapping.
> • If you enjoy the flavour and texture of dried fruit, add about 50 ml raisins, sultanas or currants to the mixture.
> • Wrap energy bars individually in clingfilm to retain crispness.

ENERGY BARS

Makes about 30 energy bars

These easy-to-make crunchy bars are a source of energy, nourishment and roughage.

50 g (50 ml) peanut butter
125 g (150 ml) butter or hard
    margarine, softened
80 g (100 ml) brown sugar
1 egg
2 ml vanilla essence
75 g (150 ml) Golden Cloud cake flour
85 g (150 ml) Golden Cloud Krakley
    Wheat wholewheat flour
50 ml wheat germ or digestive bran
45 g (150 ml) desiccated coconut
120 g (300 ml) rolled oats
50 ml sunflower seeds
50 g (25 ml) chopped pecans or walnuts
40 g (150 ml) crushed cornflakes
2 ml bicarbonate of soda
5 ml baking powder

1 Preheat the oven to 190°C. Generously grease a medium baking tray.
2 Cream together the peanut butter, butter or margarine and brown sugar in a food processor or with an electric mixer. Add the egg and vanilla essence and beat well.
3 Place the flours, wheat germ or digestive bran, coconut, rolled oats, sunflower seeds, nuts, cornflakes, bicarb and baking powder into a bowl and mix to combine evenly. Add to the creamed peanut butter mixture and mix to form a smooth dough.
4 Press the dough neatly into the baking tray. Cut into fingers (approximately 80 x 35 mm) and bake for 15 minutes until the bars are golden brown. Remove from the oven and allow the bars to cool for a short while in the tray, then cut them apart. Reduce the oven temperature to 100°C.
5 Remove from the baking tray and rearrange on the tray, slightly apart, packing them in two layers. Return to the oven for 30 minutes to dry out and become crisp. Allow to cool.

COCONUT AND OAT BARS

Makes about 32 bars, depending on size

These all-time favourites are wholesome, high-fibre energy boosters.

80 g (250 ml) desiccated coconut
100 g (250 ml) quick-cooking oats
120 g (250 ml) Golden Cloud cake flour
150 g (200 ml) sugar
5 ml bicarbonate of soda
pinch salt
125 g (150 ml) butter or hard margarine
15 ml golden syrup
15 ml water
5 ml vanilla essence

1 Preheat the oven to 180°C. Generously grease a small baking tray or ovenproof dish measuring approximately 30 x 20 cm.
2 Place the coconut, oats, flour, sugar, bicarb and salt into a mixing bowl. Mix to combine. Gently melt the butter or margarine with the syrup in a saucepan, or in a jug in the microwave on Medium; don't make it too hot. Stir in the water and vanilla essence. Add to the dry ingredients and mix well.
3 Press the mixture evenly into the prepared tray or dish. Bake for 15–20 minutes until lightly browned. Cut into bars about 75 x 25 mm. Allow to cool for about 10 minutes, and remove carefully from the tray or dish. Store in an airtight container, or wrap individually in clingfilm to retain crispness.

COOK'S NOTES
• To make the biscuits even crunchier, add up to 50 g (125 ml) chopped nuts such as pecans, brazils or unsalted mixed nuts to the dry ingredients.
• For extra-crispy biscuits, place the cut bars, slightly apart, onto a baking tray and dry them out in the oven for 20–30 minutes at 60°C, with the door slightly open.

SUGAR BISCUITS

Makes about 25 medium or 40 small biscuits

These crisp, sugary German biscuits, known as zückerkringel, *are an excellent tea-time biscuit. Alternatively, make them quite small and serve with coffee.*

125 g (150 ml) butter or hard margarine, softened
200 g (250 ml) sugar
2 ml vanilla essence
1 ml almond essence (optional)
2 eggs
250 g (500 ml) Golden Cloud cake flour
7 ml baking powder
pinch salt
80 g (100 ml) extra sugar (approximate amount)

1 Preheat the oven to 190°C. Grease two medium baking trays.
2 Beat together the butter or margarine and sugar in a food processor or with an electric mixer, until light and fluffy. Beat in the vanilla and almond essences and eggs.
3 Add the flour, baking powder and salt, and mix to a smooth dough. Pinch off small pieces about the size of heaped teaspoons (or smaller ones, half that size, if preferred) and roll into balls.
4 Put the extra sugar into a small saucer and press in the biscuits on both sides, flattening them into disks at the same time. Place onto the baking trays. Bake for about 12–15 minutes for larger biscuits, or 8–10 minutes for smaller biscuits, until golden but not too brown. Overbaking will spoil the taste and appearance of these delicate biscuits.
5 Lift the biscuits onto a wire rack; allow to cool and crisp. Store in an airtight container.

COOK'S NOTE
To make nutty biscuits mix in chopped almonds or sprinkle nuts (peanuts) with the sugar coating.

SOETKOEKIES

Makes about 36 medium soetkoekies

350 g (750 ml) Golden Cloud cake flour
5 ml ground cinnamon
5 ml ground ginger
2 ml ground mace
1 ml ground cloves
1 ml grated nutmeg
30 g (75 ml) ground almonds
pinch salt
125 g (150 ml) soft butter
125 g (150 ml) lard or schmaltz
    (or use extra butter or hard
    margarine, or a mixture)
250 g (300 ml) sugar
2 eggs
5 ml bicarbonate of soda
15 ml water
a few drops of water or extra cake flour

1 Preheat the oven to 190°C. Grease two
  medium baking trays.
2 Place the flour, cinnamon, ginger, mace,
  cloves, nutmeg, ground almonds and salt
  into a mixing bowl and stir well to combine.
3 Place the butter, fat or margarine and sugar
  into another mixing bowl, and beat until well
  creamed. Add the eggs and mix well. Dissolve
  the bicarb in the water and beat in.
4 Add the dry ingredients to the butter
  mixture. Beat or mix in, and knead lightly
  to a moderately stiff dough. Add extra water
  or flour if necessary. Form the dough into a
  ball, cover and refrigerate for 10 minutes.
5 Roll out the dough thinly (approximately
  5 mm) on a lightly floured surface. Cut out
  biscuits with round or fancy cutters, and
  place them onto the baking trays, slightly
  apart to allow for spreading.
6 Bake for 12–15 minutes until the soetkoekies
  are firm and very lightly browned around the
  edges. Lift onto a wire rack and allow
  to cool. Store in an airtight container.

DESERT DELIGHTS

Makes about 20 biscuits

*These biscuits have a sandy texture and an
unusual, cracked appearance – hence the
reference to the desert.*

1 egg
30 ml water
125 ml sunflower oil
100 g (125 ml) sugar
30 ml peanut butter
1 ml salt
2 ml ground cinnamon
1/2 ml ground cloves
1 ml almond essence
170 g (350 ml) Golden Cloud cake flour
whole blanched almonds, or walnuts,
    or pecans (one per biscuit; optional)

1 Whisk together the egg and water and set
  aside. It will be used later to bind the dough
  and glaze the biscuits.
2 Place the oil, sugar, peanut butter, salt,
  cinnamon, cloves and almond essence into a
  mixing bowl or into the bowl of a food
  processor, and beat or blend well. Add the
  flour and blend or beat to combine.
3 Gradually add just enough of the egg
  mixture to hold the dough together; don't
  make it too soft. Turn out onto a work
  surface; knead gently and form into a ball.
  Roll the dough with your palms into a neat
  roll about 25 cm long. Wrap in clingfilm
  and refrigerate for at least 1 hour to firm up.
4 Preheat the oven to 170°C. Grease a medium
  baking tray. Cut the dough neatly into
  10 mm slices, lay them onto the tray, and
  press an almond into each round.
5 Brush the dough with the remaining egg
  mixture. Bake for about 20 minutes until
  the biscuits are firm and browned around
  the edges. Switch off the oven, open the
  door partially and allow the biscuits to cool
  and crisp in the oven for 10 minutes. Place
  onto a wire rack and allow to cool.

GINGER BISCUITS

Makes about 50 biscuits

185 g (200 ml) butter or hard
    margarine, softened
80 g (100 ml) sugar
60 ml golden syrup or maple syrup
5 ml vanilla essence
5 ml ground cinnamon
2 ml ground cloves
10 ml ground ginger
2 ml grated nutmeg
5 ml bicarbonate of soda
250 g (500 ml) Golden Cloud cake flour
50 g (75 ml) extra sugar
    (approximate amount)

1 Beat together the butter or margarine and
  sugar in a food processor, or with an electric
  mixer until light and fluffy. Scrape down the
  sides of the bowl as necessary. Add all the
  remaining ingredients and mix until the
  dough holds together.
2 Remove the dough from the bowl and knead
  lightly by hand until quite smooth. Roll into
  a neat roll, about 40 mm in diameter. Wrap
  in clingfilm and refrigerate for at least
  1 hour, until firm.
3 Preheat the oven to 180°C. Grease two
  medium baking trays.
4 Cut the dough into thin slices, about 5 mm
  thick. Press both sides lightly into the extra
  sugar. Place onto the baking trays, 20 mm
  apart to allow for spreading.
5 Bake for 12–15 minutes until the biscuits are
  slightly cracked, dry, and an attractive golden
  brown colour. Don't overbake them; you'll
  spoil the flavour.
6 Lift the biscuits onto a wire rack and allow
  to cool and become firm and crisp. Store in
  an airtight container.

> ### COOK'S NOTE
> The dough may be chilled, rolled out thinly,
> cut into fancy shapes, and decorated. Or,
> cut into rounds (40–60 mm in diameter)
> to serve with dessert.

DUTCH BUTTER BISCUITS

Makes about 24 biscuits

Scrumptious biscuits from Dutch kitchens to add to your list of family favourites.

125 g (150 ml) butter or hard
   margarine, softened
60 g (75 ml) castor sugar
2 ml vanilla essence
1 egg yolk
180 g (375 ml) Golden Cloud cake flour
TOPPING
24 blanched almonds
   (approximate amount)
1 egg white
castor sugar for sprinkling

1 Preheat the oven to 180°C. Grease two
   medium baking trays.
2 Beat together the butter, castor sugar and
   vanilla essence in a food processor, or with
   an electric mixer until creamy. Beat in the
   egg yolk. Add the flour and beat lightly just
   until a dough is formed.
3 Gently work the mixture by hand until the
   dough is smooth. Break off pieces about the
   size of walnuts and roll into balls. Place
   them onto the baking trays, about 25 mm
   apart to a low for spreading. Press an
   almond firmly into the centre of each. Beat
   the egg white lightly and brush onto each
   biscuit. Sprinkle with castor sugar.
4 Bake for 18–20 minutes until the biscuits
   are pale golden. Transfer onto a wire rack
   and allow to cool.

COOK'S NOTES
• To make crescent-shaped butter biscuits,
roll the dough balls into ropes. Press the
ropes into nibbed almonds, if you wish. Twist
gently into crescent shapes, place onto
baking trays and bake as instructed.
• The dough makes a delicious sweet pie
crust. Press evenly into a greased pie plate
and bake blind (see page 8).

SEMOLINA BISCUIT FINGERS

Makes about 18 biscuits

150 g (300 ml) Golden Cloud cake flour
pinch salt
50 g (75 ml) Golden Cloud semolina
100 g (100 ml) butter or hard
    margarine, cut into cubes
80 g (100 ml) castor sugar
1 egg yolk
2 ml vanilla essence
2 drops almond essence (optional)
TOPPING
1 egg white
castor sugar for sprinkling

1 Preheat the oven to 160°C. Grease a small baking tray or ovenproof dish (30 x 20 cm).
2 Place the flour, salt and semolina into a mixing bowl, or the bowl of a food processor and mix until combined. Add the butter or margarine, and mix or process until the mixture is crumbly.
3 Add the castor sugar, egg yolk and vanilla and almond essences, and mix or process until the dough just holds together; do not overmix.
4 Press the dough evenly into the prepared dish or baking tray, and prick decoratively with a fork. Lightly beat the egg white and brush onto the pastry. Sprinkle with sugar.
5 Bake for about 20 minutes until pale golden. Switch off the oven, leaving the door partially open, and leave the biscuits for 10 minutes to crisp.
6 Cut the biscuits into neat fingers. Lift carefully onto a wire rack and allow to cool and crisp. Store in an airtight container.

COOK'S NOTES
• For roasted almond biscuits, scatter flaked almonds on top and press them lightly into the dough before brushing with egg white.
• To make nutty biscuits, add 50 g coarsely chopped, roasted hazelnuts (see page 12) to dry ingredients and increase butter or margarine to 125 g (150 ml).

SNICKERDOODLES

Makes about 25 biscuits

Plain but flavourful crunchy biscuits of German origin.

125 ml sunflower oil
125 g (150 ml) sugar
1 egg
170 g (350 ml) Golden Cloud cake flour
1 ml grated nutmeg (optional)
pinch salt
7 ml cream of tartar
2 ml bicarbonate of soda
COATING
30 ml sugar
5 ml ground cinnamon

1 Place the oil, sugar and egg into a mixing bowl, or the bowl of a food processor and beat well. Add the flour, nutmeg, salt, cream of tartar and bicarb, and blend or beat well until the dough holds together. Knead lightly by hand until smooth, then cover and refrigerate for 30–60 minutes.
2 Preheat the oven to 190°C. Grease two medium baking trays. Mix together in a small bowl the sugar and cinnamon.
3 Pinch off pieces of dough and shape into walnut-sized balls. Roll them in the cinnamon sugar and place onto the baking tray, about 50 mm apart. Flatten very slightly with your thumb. Bake for about 10 minutes until the biscuits are lightly browned.
4 Allow to cool on a wire rack.

CHOCOLATE SHORTBREAD

Makes about 24 medium shortbread fingers

These rich chocolate bars are popular for home industries, as they pack neatly for display purposes. For special occasions the edges can be dipped into melted white chocolate.

350 g (400 ml) butter or hard
    margarine, cut into cubes
    and softened
150 g (200 ml) caramel sugar
400 g (800 ml) Golden Cloud cake flour
pinch salt
50 g (150 ml) cocoa powder
30 ml milk (approximate amount)
castor sugar for sprinkling
CHOCOLATE COATING (OPTIONAL)
200 g white chocolate

1 Preheat the oven to 180°C. Generously grease a small baking tray or overproof dish (30 x 20 cm).
2 Place the butter or margarine, sugar, flour, salt, cocoa and milk into the bowl of an electric mixer fitted with the batter hook. Mix, adding the milk drop by drop until the dough holds together. If preparing by hand or with a hand beater, cream together the butter or margarine and sugar. Add the remaining ingredients and mix and knead by hand to a firm dough. Add just enough milk, drop by drop, to bind the dough.
3 Press and roll out the dough evenly in the baking tray or dish. Prick neatly with a fork. Bake for about 25 minutes until the shortbread is cooked and firm.
4 Allow to cool for a few minutes in the baking tray, then cut into fingers or squares and sprinkle with castor sugar. Remove carefully and place onto a wire rack to cool.
5 If coating with chocolate, cut the biscuits into fingers; don't sprinkle with castor sugar. Melt the chocolate (see page 11). Dip the short edge of each biscuit into the chocolate. Place onto a wire rack to cool. Store in airtight containers.

COOK'S NOTE
If you don't wish to make classic shortbread fingers, the dough can be rolled out on a floured surface to a thickness of about 50 mm and cut into fancy shapes. Handle with care, as the dough is fragile. Place onto greased baking trays and bake for about 15 minutes until the biscuits are firm. Allow to cool. Coat each biscuit with melted chocolate and decorate with chocolate vermicelli, hundreds and thousands or roasted nuts.

WHITE CHOCOLATE AND MACADAMIA BISCUITS

Makes about 24 biscuits, depending on size

200 g white chocolate
100 g (200 ml) macadamia nuts
125 g (140 ml) butter or hard
    margarine, softened
125 g (150 ml) caramel sugar,
    or half white, half caramel sugar
1 egg
5 ml vanilla essence
180 g (375 ml) Golden Cloud cake flour
2 ml baking powder
2 ml bicarbonate of soda
pinch salt

1 Preheat the oven to 190°C. Grease two medium baking trays.
2 Break the chocolate into blocks and chop coarsely. Chop the nuts very coarsely.
3 Place the butter or margarine, sugar/s, egg and vanilla essence into the bowl of a food processor and beat until light and creamy. Scrape down the sides if necessary. Alternatively, beat together the butter or margarine and the sugar/s in a bowl until light and fluffy. Add the egg and vanilla essence and beat until creamy.
4 Add the flour, baking powder, bicarb and salt, and blend or beat until evenly combined. Stir in the chopped chocolate and nuts.
5 Place heaped teaspoons of dough onto the baking trays, at least 50 mm apart to allow for spreading. Bake for 10–12 minutes until the biscuits are golden brown.
6 Allow to cool on the baking trays for a few minutes to become firm. Lift onto a wire rack and allow to cool.

COOK'S NOTE
Use milk or dark chocolate in place of white chocolate, and replace macadamias with brazil nuts, almonds, pecans, unsalted pistachios or mixed nuts, if you wish.

GOURMET CHOC-NUT BARS

Makes about 30 medium slices,
or 50 small squares

Enjoy these with coffee to end a special meal.

100 g (200 ml) Golden Cloud cake flour
1 ml baking powder
50 g (50 ml) butter or hard margarine
40 ml icing sugar
1 egg
few drops water if necessary
CHOC-NUT TOPPING
100 g (100 ml) butter or hard
    margarine, softened
175 g (200 ml) castor sugar
1 egg
5 ml vanilla essence
60 ml milk
150 g (300 ml) Golden Cloud cake flour
35 g (60 ml) ground almonds
100 g dark chocolate, roughly chopped
75 g (125 ml) seedless raisins
100 g (250 ml) roasted nuts, coarsely
    chopped (see Cook's notes)
icing sugar for dusting

1 Preheat the oven to 180°C. Grease a small
  ovenproof dish or baking tray.
2 To make the pastry: place all the ingredients
  into the bowl of a food processor, and
  process until the dough holds together,
  adding a few drops of water if necessary.
  If making the pastry by hand or in an electric
  mixer, mix and knead the ingredients
  together to form a dough.
3 Press the pastry evenly to line the base of
  the dish or tray. Bake for 10 minutes until
  just firm and very pale golden.
4 To make the choc-nut topping, place the
  butter or margarine, castor sugar, egg,
  vanilla essence, milk, flour and ground
  almonds into the bowl of a food processor,
  and process to a smooth batter. If making
  by hand or in an electric mixer, beat together
  the butter or margarine and castor sugar
  until creamy. Beat in the egg, vanilla essence

and milk. Add the flour and almonds, and
beat until smooth.
5 Add the chocolate, raisins and nuts, and stir
  in until well combined. Spoon the mixture
  onto the baked pastry and spread evenly.
  Reduce the oven temperature to 160°C and
  bake for about 25 minutes, until the topping
  is golden and set.
6 Allow to cool for 5 minutes before cutting
  into neat slices or squares. Dust with icing
  sugar. Allow to cool for a few minutes more,
  then lift onto a wire rack to cool completely.

COOK'S NOTES
• Mix shelled hazelnuts, blanched almonds
  and pistachios for the best results,
  or substitute unsalted mixed nuts.
  Roast the nuts (see page 12) and chop.
• To make individual Choc-nut Tartlets,
  generously grease 24 mini-muffin tins,
  and line them with the pastry. Spoon the
  filling into the raw pastry cups, and bake at
  180°C for about 20 minutes, until golden and
  firm. Allow to cool in the tins for a few
  minutes, then remove carefully and cool on a
  wire rack. Dust with icing sugar.

BISCOTTI

Makes about 30 biscotti

Dip into coffee or chilled dessert wine or sherry, as is Italian custom.

1 egg
1 egg white
125 ml sunflower oil
150 g (200 ml) sugar
5 ml vanilla essence
100 g (250 ml) coarsely chopped nuts
   (see Cook's notes)
200 g (400 ml) Golden Cloud cake flour
1 ml salt
5 ml aniseed (optional, but delicious)
7 ml baking powder

1 Place the egg, egg white, oil, sugar and vanilla essence into the bowl of an electric mixer, and mix until well blended. Add the nuts, flour, salt, aniseed and baking powder, and mix well to a soft, smooth dough. Cover the bowl and refrigerate for at least 2 hours, but preferably overnight. This retains a neat shape and makes the dough firm and more manageable, and prevents the dough from spreading while baking.

2 Preheat the oven to 180°C. Grease a medium baking tray. Divide the dough into two and shape each portion into a neat roll about 30 cm long. Place onto the prepared tray, allowing space in between for spreading.

3 Reduce the oven temperature to 160°C and bake for about 20 minutes until the biscotti rolls are quite firm and lightly browned. The rolls will spread out slightly while baking. Remove the tray from the oven and reduce the oven temperature to 100°C.

4 Cut each roll diagonally into 15 mm slices. Lay each slice on its side on the baking tray, and return to the oven. Leave the door slightly ajar to allow the moisture to escape. Leave the biscotti in the oven for 20–30 minutes until dry, crisp and lightly browned. Switch off the oven and allow them to cool completely in the oven.

BISCOTTI VARIATIONS

Choc-chip or Nutty Choc-chip Biscotti
Use tiny chocolate chips, weight for weight, instead of some or all of the nuts. Chocolate combines well with lightly roasted slivered almonds.

Coffee-cashew Biscotti
Add 5 ml instant coffee granules to the egg mixture, and use coarsely chopped unsalted cashew nuts.

Coconut or Choc-coconut Biscotti
Replace some or all of the nuts, weight for weight, with desiccated coconut, or desiccated coconut combined with chocolate chips.

Lemon Biscotti
Substitute 10 ml finely grated lemon zest for the vanilla essence and aniseed, and use any nuts of your choice.

Cereal Biscotti
Replace all or some of the nuts, weight for weight, with cornflakes or quick-cooking oats. Lightly brown the oats in a little butter or margarine and allow to cool before adding to the dough.

FAT-FREE BISCOTTI

Makes about 30 biscotti

Excellent for those on a low-fat regime, and an opportunity to use up extra egg whites.

125 ml egg white (of 4–5 eggs)
150 g (175 ml) castor sugar
2 ml vanilla essence
100 g (200 ml) Golden Cloud cake flour
pinch salt
100 g (250 ml) nuts (see Cook's notes)

1 Preheat the oven to 180°C. Line the base and sides of a medium (26 cm) loaf tin with baking paper and grease well.

2 Place the egg white into a mixing bowl, or the bowl of an electric mixer fitted with the balloon whisk, and beat until stiff peaks form. Add the castor sugar gradually, whipping until thick and glossy, as for meringue. Beat in the vanilla essence.

3 Add the flour, salt and nuts, and fold in very lightly with the whisk or a large spoon until just combined (don't overmix). Pour into the prepared tin, smooth the top and bake for about 25 minutes until firm and golden. Allow to cool, then loosen and turn out onto a wire rack to cool completely.

4 Preheat the oven to 100°C. Slice the loaf into 5 mm slices using an electric knife or sharp, serrated knife. Arrange flat onto a baking tray. Return the biscotti to the oven, leaving the door slightly ajar, for about 20 minutes, turning over once, until crisp and dry. Allow the biscotti to cool on a wire rack. Store in airtight containers.

COOK'S NOTES
• To make very small biscotti, divide the dough into three sections before rolling and baking.
• Use one type of nut, or combine several, such as pecans, walnuts, hazelnuts, slivered almonds or unsalted cashews. To roast, see page 12.

RICH BUTTERMILK RUSKS WITH SESAME SEEDS

Makes about 50 rusks

1 kg (1.8 litres) Golden Cloud
   self-raising flour
10 ml baking powder
5 ml salt
5 ml aniseed (optional)
200 g (250 ml) sugar
80 g (250 ml) desiccated coconut,
   or 80 g (200 ml) ground almonds
250 g (280 ml) butter or hard
   margarine, cut into cubes
250 ml sour cream
250 ml buttermilk
2 eggs, lightly beaten
GLAZE
1 egg
30 ml milk
30 ml sesame seeds

COOK'S NOTE
Instead of making it into balls, divide the dough in half and press evenly into two large greased baking trays. Cut into neat fingers, brush with glaze and sprinkle with sesame seeds. Bake for about 30 minutes until golden and firm. Allow to cool in the tins. Cut or break into fingers.

1 Preheat the oven to 180°C. Generously grease an oven roasting pan (35 x 25 cm), or two large (28 cm) loaf tins.
2 Place the flour, baking powder, salt, aniseed, sugar and coconut or almonds into a large mixing bowl. Add the butter or margarine. Rub in with your fingertips and between your palms until the mixture is coarsely crumbled. Make a well in the centre.
3 Add the sour cream, buttermilk and eggs, and mix to a soft dough. Turn out onto a floured surface and knead lightly until smooth. Pinch off bits of dough the size of golf balls, and pack them – just touching – into the prepared pan or tins.
4 Beat together the egg and milk for the glaze, and brush onto the rusks. Sprinkle with sesame seeds. Bake for about 45 minutes, until the rusks are golden brown and firm, and a cake-tester comes out clean.
5 Allow the rusks to cool in the pan or tins for a short while, then turn out onto a wire rack to cool completely. Break apart and pack onto baking trays, with space in between. Place in a very low oven (60°C) for about 6 hours, until completely crisp and dry. Leave the door slightly ajar for moisture to escape. When quite dry, allow the rusks to cool completely on a wire rack. Store in airtight containers for up to a month.

COUNTRY CREAM RUSKS

Makes about 100 rusks

1 kg (1.8 litres) Golden Cloud
   self-raising flour
200 g (250 ml) sugar
5 ml salt
10 ml aniseed (optional)
2 eggs
1 litre cream (approximate amount)

1 Preheat the oven to 180°C. Generously grease two large (28 cm) loaf tins.
2 Combine the flour, sugar, salt and aniseed in a mixing bowl. Make a well in the centre. Add the eggs and about three quarters of the cream. Mix lightly by hand to break up the eggs, then mix well, adding enough of the remaining cream to form a dough that is neither too firm nor too soft.
3 Turn the dough out onto a floured surface and knead lightly for a few minutes until smooth. Pinch off pieces about the size of golf balls, and roll into slightly elongated shapes. Pack into the greased tins in neat rows, just touching each other.
4 Bake for about 35 minutes until golden brown and firm, and a cake-tester comes out clean. Reduce the oven temperature slightly if the tops brown too much or too soon, and cover loosely with foil if necessary.
5 Allow to cool in the tins for a few minutes, then turn out onto a wire rack. Turn over and cool completely. Cover with a kitchen cloth and set aside for at least 2–3 hours before breaking into rusks. If broken apart too soon, they will be very crumbly.
6 Pack loosely onto baking trays and dry out at 60°C for 5–6 hours. Leave the door slightly ajar. When quite dry, cool the rusks on a wire rack. Store for up to a month.

COOK'S NOTE
Create variations by adding 125 ml sunflower seeds fried in a dash of oil and cooled, or 125 ml desiccated coconut or mixed seeds (sesame, poppy, sunflower and linseeds).

CONDENSED MILK RUSKS

Makes about 120 rusks

These South African favourites are made with yeast, have a fine texture and superb flavour, and are the easiest yeast rusks to make. For a special treat, break off the freshly baked rusks and spread with butter.

397 g tin full-cream condensed milk
100 g (125 ml) sugar
125 g (150 ml) butter or hard
    margarine, cut into cubes and
    softened
15 ml salt
15 ml aniseed (optional)
250 ml boiling water
500 ml lukewarm water
2 eggs
1–2 x 10 g sachets instant yeast
    (see Cook's notes)
1.2 kg (2.5 litres or 10 x 250 ml cups)
    Golden Cloud cake flour
    (approximate amount)

1 Place the condensed milk, sugar, butter or margarine, salt and aniseed into a large mixing bowl, or the bowl of an electric mixer. Rinse out the condensed milk tin with the boiling water, and add it to the mixing bowl. Stir until the condensed milk, butter or margarine and sugar have melted.

2 Add the lukewarm water, mix in well and allow to cool. Add the eggs. Mix the yeast with 120 g (250 ml) of the flour and add to the bowl. Add about half the remaining flour and mix well. Gradually add enough of the remaining flour to form a soft dough.

3 If using an electric mixer, fit the dough hook, cover the bowl with the splashguard or a cloth, and move the mixer to the back of the worktop to prevent it from moving to the edge while kneading. Knead for 5–7 minutes. Finish by kneading lightly by hand on a floured surface, adding a little extra flour to obtain a smooth, nonsticky dough. To knead by hand, turn out the dough onto a floured surface and knead for 8–10 minutes, adding a little extra flour, if and when necessary, to obtain a soft, yet smooth, elastic dough.

4 Flour the bowl lightly, place the dough into the bowl, sprinkle with flour, cover and set aside in a very warm spot until doubled in bulk. This will take 1–2 hours, depending on the amount of yeast and the temperature of the room.

5 Generously grease three large (28 cm) or four medium (26 cm) loaf tins. Knead the dough lightly and pinch off pieces the size of golf balls. Pack tightly together into the tins, which should be about one-third full to allow for expansion and feather-light rusks.

6 Cover the tins and place in a draft-free, warm spot, and allow the dough to rise slowly and neatly out of the tins. If the dough is left to rise in a spot that is too warm, it will rise unevenly, and the texture of the rusks will be spoilt.

7 Preheat the oven to 160°C. Bake the rusks, allowing space between the tins for the heat to circulate, for 35–40 minutes until well risen and golden brown. A cake-tester will come out clean, and they will sound hollow when tapped. If they brown too quickly, cover loosely with foil and reduce the temperature to 150°C.

8 Turn the rusks out onto a wire rack. The underside should be light golden and firm. If the rusks are too pale and soft, return them to the tins and bake a short while longer. Turn the baked rusk loaves over and allow to cool upright for at least 1 hour. Reduce the oven temperature to 60°C.

9 Turn the loaves over and break the rusks apart from base to top – this way they won't break at the base, where they are more firmly attached. Pack onto baking trays in two layers if necessary, allowing sufficient space in between for air circulation.

10 Place the rusks into the oven, with the door slightly open for moisture to escape, for 6–8 hours until completely dry but not browned. Allow to cool on wire racks. Store in airtight containers.

COOK'S NOTES
- When time is tight or the weather is cold, use 2 sachets of instant yeast for quick and efficient rising. In warmer weather, 1 sachet will rise the dough within about two hours, and the rusks within one hour.
- Aniseed is the traditional flavouring, but leave it out if you're not mad about it. The rusks will still taste great.
Rusks may be stored up to a month or even longer in airtight containers; perfect for holidays, hostel food and hungry students.

CRUNCHY BRAN AND SEED RUSKS

Makes about 100 rusks

Wholesome, grainy rusks with a delightfully coarse, yet light and crumbly texture.

1 kg (2 litres) Golden Cloud cake flour
60 ml baking powder
10 ml salt
150 g (750 ml) digestive bran
400 g (500 ml) sugar
100 g (200 ml) sunflower seeds
60 g (100 ml) poppy seeds
60 g (200 ml) desiccated coconut,
  or 70 g (200 ml) oats
500 g (560 ml) butter or hard
  margarine, cut into cubes
1 litre buttermilk
4 eggs, lightly beaten

1 Preheat the oven to 180°C. Generously grease three large (28 cm) loaf tins or four medium (26 cm) loaf tins.
2 Place the flour, baking powder, salt, digestive bran, sugar, seeds, and coconut or oats into a large mixing bowl, and stir to combine. Make a well in the centre.
3 Melt the butter or margarine in a saucepan over medium heat, or in a jug in the microwave on Medium; don't make it too hot. Add, together with the buttermilk and eggs, to the dry ingredients. Stir until you have a well-mixed, heavy batter.
4 Spoon the batter into the prepared tins and bake for about 50 minutes until firm and browned, and a cake-tester comes out clean.
5 Allow the rusks to cool in the tins for 5 minutes, then turn out onto a wire rack and allow to cool completely – for at least an hour, preferably longer. Cut into thick slices, and then into fingers with a sharp, serrated knife, or an electric knife.
6 Arrange the rusks on baking trays with spaces in between. Place in a very low oven (60°C) for about 6–8 hours, until completely crisp and dry. Allow to cool.

> ### COOK'S NOTE
> For wholewheat bran rusks without seeds, omit the seeds and add 140 g (250 ml) Golden Cloud Krakley Wheat wholewheat flour to the dry ingredients.

BRAN AND MUESLI RUSK FINGERS

Makes about 60 rusks

Delicious rusks packed with fibre, goodness and flavour.

1 kg (1.8 litres) Golden Cloud
  self-raising flour
140 g (250 ml) Golden Cloud Krakley
  Wheat wholewheat flour
100 g (750 ml) bran flakes
125 g (250 ml) toasted or plain muesli
200 g (250 ml) sugar
5 ml salt
5 ml baking powder
400 g (450 ml) butter or hard
  margarine, cut into cubes
200 ml sunflower oil
500 ml buttermilk
3 eggs, lightly beaten

1 Preheat the oven to 180°C. Grease two medium baking trays.
2 Combine the flours, bran flakes, muesli, sugar, salt and baking powder in a mixing bowl. Make a well in the centre. Melt the butter or margarine in a saucepan over medium heat or in a jug in the microwave on Medium; don't make it too hot. Add to the dry ingredients, together with the oil, buttermilk and eggs. Mix to a soft dough.
3 Press the dough evenly into the baking trays. Cut into fingers and bake for about 30 minutes until golden and firm but not too dry. Allow to cool in the tins.
4 Cut or break the rusks into fingers. Place onto baking trays with space in between and dry out in a very low oven (60°C) for about 6 hours, until crisp. Leave the oven door slightly ajar. Allow the rusks to cool.

> ### COOK'S NOTE
> For a yummy variation, add mixed seeds (100 ml sunflower seeds, 50 ml sesame seeds and 30 ml linseeds) to the dry ingredients.

SCONES
MUFFINS
& PANCAKES

These recipes are the essence of homely cooking, and are quick and easy to make – perfect for first-time bakers and children yearning to get stuck into the kitchen. Besides being versatile enough to serve casually or include on an elegant menu, no bazaar, flea market or school fete would be complete without home-made muffins, and a pancake stall with wafting aromas of sizzling batter and cinnamon sugar.

Scone dough is wonderfully flexible, resulting in treats ranging from utterly simple to deliciously rich. And, by adding or substituting ingredients, many flavour and texture variations are possible. Handle scone dough lightly; heavy kneading will spoil the light, crumbly texture. And home-made scones, served warm or cool, deserve nothing but the best jam or preserves, and whipped cream or grated cheese.

Muffins – sweet and savoury – are extraordinarily popular, and can be small or medium, jumbo or extra jumbo in size. There's no special trick to success, but never overmix the batter, as this makes them tough. Batter for 12 medium muffins will make eight jumbo (200 ml muffin cups) or 36 mini muffins. Bake jumbos slightly longer than the specified time, and minis for about two-thirds of the baking time.

Crumpets are the friendliest of tea-time treats. Try the wholewheat version with sweet or savoury toppings, or with a sauce, for breakfast, as a snack, or as a starter before a meal.

Waffle irons have become high tech these days, and those with a nonstick coating are great. Waffles must be served immediately, so gather everyone around the kitchen counter for a relaxing get-together. You'll never serve frozen waffles again!

Cheesy Bacon and Onion Scones page 31

Savoury Scone Wheel page 31

Plain Scones page 30

PLAIN SCONES

Makes 15–20 scones

350 g (750 ml) Golden Cloud cake flour
17 ml baking powder
2 ml salt
20 ml sugar
100 g (100 ml) cold butter
    or hard margarine, cut into cubes
3 eggs
150 ml milk

1 Preheat the oven to 220°C. Grease a medium baking tray.
2 Place the flour, baking powder, salt and sugar into a mixing bowl. Add the butter or margarine, and rub in with your fingertips until crumbly. Make a well in the centre.
3 Beat together the eggs and milk. Reserve 50 ml of the mixture for glazing. Pour the egg mixture into the dry ingredients, and mix with a fork for about 30 seconds until the dough holds together. Turn out onto a lightly floured surface and knead gently and quickly, for no more than 1 minute, until the dough is smooth and no longer sticky.
4 Roll out with a floured rolling pin on a floured surface, to a thickness of about 2.5 cm. Cut out with a lightly floured cutter, 6–8 cm in diameter. Cut as close together as possible to prevent having to reroll the dough too often.
5 Place the scones, slightly apart, onto the baking tray, and brush with the reserved egg and milk glaze. Place into the oven, and reduce the temperature to 200°C. Bake for about 15 minutes, until the scones are well-risen and golden. Break one open to determine whether or not it is done. Allow to cool on a wire rack.

CHOC-CHIP NUTTY TOFFEE SCONES

Makes 10–12 servings, depending on shape and size

A special sweet treat for young and old to serve at any time of the day.

180 g (375 ml) Golden Cloud cake flour
50 ml sugar
10 ml baking powder
1 ml salt
60 g (100 ml) chocolate chips
50 g (100 ml) finely diced soft toffees
50 g (125 ml) chopped pecan nuts
250 ml cream
15 ml melted butter or hard margarine
15 ml sugar

1 Preheat the oven to 190°C. Grease a medium baking tray.
2 Place the flour, sugar, baking powder, salt, chocolate chips, toffees and nuts into a mixing bowl. Stir to combine thoroughly. Add the cream and mix with a fork to a dough.
3 Knead gently until smooth, and shape the dough in one of the following ways:
(a) Shape into a flat dome, about 3 cm thick, and place onto the baking tray. Mark into 8 wedges with the back of a large knife, brush with the melted butter or margarine and sprinkle with sugar. (b) Roll out on a lightly floured surface to a thickness of 3 cm, and cut into circles about 3–4 cm in diameter, or into fingers about 2 cm wide. Place onto the baking tray, slightly apart. Brush with melted butter or margarine, and sprinkle with sugar.
4 Bake for about 20 minutes until the scones are well-risen and light golden brown. Allow to cool on a wire rack. Serve warm with butter, or cool completely and store in an airtight container.

COOK'S NOTES
• These scones freeze very well. Thaw and reheat for a few minutes at 160°C, or in the microwave on Defrost for about 30 seconds per scone.
• To make savoury scones, decrease the sugar to 15 ml and replace the chocolate chips, nuts and toffee with about 300 ml of a savoury mixture (grated cheese, chopped ham, cooked or tinned corn kernels, chopped spring onion, fried onion or green pepper, chopped fresh herbs or dried herbs, or garlic and herb seasoning). Replace the sugar topping with coarse salt.
• Make toasted cheese scones with day-old savoury scones. Slice 3–4 scones in half and place onto a baking tray. Mix about 150 g (375 ml) grated cheddar cheese with an egg, a dash of dry or prepared mustard, and a little chopped spring onion. Spoon onto the scone halves, shaping evenly. Dust with Red Sprinkle Mix (page 12), and grill until the topping is brown and bubbly.

COOK'S NOTES
• Scones can be stored for no longer than a day in an airtight container. Freshen up by loosely covering with light foil and reheating for 6–8 minutes at 160°C, or halve and toast them.
• Any scone dough lends itself to interesting variations, some of which are offered in the Scone Variations on page 31.

RICH BUTTERMILK SCONES

Makes 15–20 scones

350 g (750 ml) Golden Cloud cake flour
25 ml baking powder
2 ml salt
15 ml sugar
2 eggs
200 ml cream
200 ml buttermilk
water to dilute glaze

1 Preheat the oven to 220°C. Grease a medium baking tray.
2 Place the flour, baking powder, salt and sugar into a mixing bowl, and stir until evenly blended. Make a well in the centre.
3 Beat together the eggs, cream and buttermilk. Reserve 30 ml of this mixture for glazing. Pour the liquid into the dry ingredients and mix with a fork until the dough holds together. Turn the soft, sticky dough onto a well-floured surface, and knead lightly with floured hands for no more than 1 minute. Add a little extra flour if necessary, to form a very soft, pliable, smooth dough.
4 Roll out with a floured rolling pin on a floured surface to a thickness of 2.5 cm, and cut out neat rounds, 5–8 cm in diameter, with a scone cutter. Cut out as close together as possible to prevent having to reroll the dough too often.
5 Place the scones, slightly apart, onto the baking tray. Dilute the reserved egg mixture with a little water, and brush onto the scones.
6 Bake for 10–15 minutes, depending on size, until the scones are well-risen and golden. Break one open to determine whether or not it is done. Allow to cool on a wire rack.

COOK'S NOTE
Rich buttermilk scones remain moist for up to three days in an airtight container, preferably in the fridge. Freshen by reheating, loosely covered with light foil, for a few minutes at 160°C.

SCONE VARIATIONS
Use the basic recipe for Plain Scones (page 30) or Rich Buttermilk Scones

Wholewheat Scones
Substitute one-third to two-thirds of the cake flour with wholewheat flour. Add any of the ingredients below to make savoury or sweet wholewheat scones.

Cheese Scones
Add 100 g (250 ml) grated cheddar or other tasty cheese, 5 ml dry English mustard, and milled black pepper or cayenne pepper to the dry ingredients after rubbing in the butter or margarine. Lightly dust the glazed scones with Red Sprinkle Mix (page 12), or garlic and herb seasoning.

Cheesy Bacon and Onion Scones
Add about 100 ml chopped, cooked bacon, pepper ham or salami, and about 30 ml chopped spring onion to Cheese Scones.

Herbed Scones
Add 30 ml chopped, mixed fresh herbs or 5 ml dried mixed herbs, and 20 ml each chopped fresh parsley and finely snipped spring onion tips to the dry ingredients.

Savoury Scone Wheel
Mix 200 g (500 ml) grated cheddar cheese or other tasty cheese, 50 ml chopped cooked bacon or ham, 10 ml dry English mustard, 30 ml finely chopped onion and 15 ml chopped fresh parsley. Divide the scone dough in half, and roll out into two circles, each about 10 cm thick. Sprinkle the savoury mix onto one; cover with the other circle and press down lightly. Place onto a greased baking tray, and mark about 12–16 wedges with the back of a knife, cutting almost through. Brush with egg and milk glaze, and dust with Red Sprinkle Mix (page 12), or garlic and herb seasoning.

Fruit Scones
Add 125–250 ml sultanas, raisins or other dried fruit to the crumbly mixture.

Sesame Scone Fingers
Roll out the scone dough into a 40 x 20 cm rectangle. Cut in half lengthways, then into 10 strips across to make about 20 fingers. Melt 50 g (50 ml) butter or hard margarine and pour onto a plate. Sprinkle 50 ml sesame seeds onto another plate. Roll each dough finger into the butter or margarine, then into the seeds. Arrange, almost touching, on a greased baking tray, and bake for about 15 minutes until the scones are golden and a cake-tester comes out clean.

Drop Scones
Add about 100 ml extra water or milk to any of the scone variations to create a heavy batter. Drop spoonfuls onto the baking tray and bake for about 15 minutes until a cake-tester comes out clean.

EVERYDAY MUFFINS

Makes 12 medium muffins

Marvellous, melt-in-the-mouth muffins.

350 g (750 ml) Golden Cloud cake flour
40 ml sugar
15 ml baking powder
2 ml salt
125 g (150 ml) butter or hard margarine
2 eggs
350 ml milk

1 Preheat the oven to 200°C. Grease 12 cups of a standard muffin tin, greasing on top between the cups as well.
2 Place the flour, sugar, baking powder and salt into a mixing bowl, and stir until evenly combined. Make a well in the centre.
3 Melt the butter or margarine in a small saucepan, or in a jug in the microwave on Medium; don't make it too hot.
4 Beat together the eggs and milk, and add to the dry ingredients together with the melted butter or margarine. Stir to combine. Don't overmix. Divide the batter between the muffin cups and bake for about 20 minutes until the muffins are golden, and a cake-tester comes out clean.
5 Allow to cool in the tin for a few minutes, then loosen, lift out carefully and place onto a wire rack to cool. Serve with butter and any sweet or savoury accompaniment.

EVERYDAY MUFFIN VARIATIONS

Seed Muffins
Add 15 ml sesame seeds, 15 ml poppy seeds and 3 ml aniseed to dry ingredients. Sprinkle the muffins with a mix of 5 ml sesame seeds and 5 ml poppy seeds.

Cheese Muffins
Add 150 g (375 ml) grated cheddar or emmental to the dry ingredients. Add 20 ml poppy seeds, if you wish. Serve with cream cheese and smoked salmon or trout.

POPPY SEED NUT MUFFINS

Makes 12 medium muffins

A local magazine tracked down this blissful recipe to a hotel in Disney World; the chef was thrilled to share his recipe.

80 ml flaked or slivered almonds, or coarsely chopped brazils, hazelnuts, macadamias or mixed nuts
50 ml poppy seeds
50 ml lemon juice
350 g (750 ml) Golden Cloud cake flour
15 ml baking powder
2 ml salt
50 ml sugar
75 g (75 ml) butter or hard margarine
350 ml milk
1 ml almond essence
2 eggs

1 Place the almonds and poppy seeds into a small bowl. Stir in the lemon juice. Set aside to soak for at least 15 minutes.
2 Preheat the oven to 200°C. Grease 12 cups of a standard muffin tin, greasing on top between the cups as well.
3 Place the flour, baking powder, salt and sugar into a mixing bowl, and stir until evenly combined. Make a well in the centre.
4 Melt the butter or margarine in a small saucepan, or in a jug in the microwave on Medium; don't make it too hot.
5 Beat together the milk, almond essence and eggs and pour into the dry ingredients. Add the soaked nuts and seeds, and the melted butter or margarine. Stir together to combine. Don't overmix. Divide the batter between the muffin cups and bake for about 20 minutes until the muffins are golden and a cake-tester comes out clean.
6 Allow the muffins to cool in the tin for a few minutes, then loosen, lift out carefully and place onto a wire rack to cool. Serve slightly warm or cold, with butter and jam, cheese or cream cheese.

BANANA PECAN BRAN MUFFINS

Makes 12 medium muffins

Quick, healthy, flavourful treats, and a great way of using very ripe bananas.

100 g (100 ml) butter or hard margarine
100 g (250 ml) pecan nuts (or toasted muesli, if preferred)
140 g (250 ml) Golden Cloud Krakley Wheat wholewheat flour
70 g (125 ml) Golden Cloud self-raising flour
70 g (350 ml) digestive bran
80 g (100 ml) sugar
5 ml bicarbonate of soda
1 ml salt
1 ml ground cinnamon
6 very ripe large bananas, peeled and mashed
1 egg
125 ml buttermilk

1 Preheat the oven to 200°C. Generously grease 12 cups of a standard muffin tin.
2 Melt the butter or margarine in a small saucepan, or in a jug in the microwave on Medium; don't make it too hot.
3 Reserve 12 of the pecans. Coarsely chop the remainder. Place into a bowl and add the flours, digestive bran, sugar, bicarb, salt and cinnamon. Make a well in the centre. Add the banana, melted butter or margarine, egg and buttermilk, and stir until evenly blended.
4 Divide the batter between the muffin cups and bake for about 20 minutes, until the muffins are golden brown and a cake-tester comes out clean.
5 Loosen carefully; lift onto a wire rack to cool.

> ### COOK'S NOTES
> • Banana muffins freeze very well. Thaw and warm slightly before serving.
> • If you don't have 6 bananas, substitute 50 ml extra buttermilk for each banana omitted. However, don't use less than 2 bananas.

CAPPUCCINO MUFFINS

Makes 12 medium muffins

These light, luxurious treats are a cross between a muffin and a cup cake. Fill with whipped cream for tea.

100 g (100 ml) butter or hard margarine, softened
150 g (200 ml) sugar
30 ml coffee granules
2 eggs
250 ml sour cream
5 ml vanilla essence
250 g (500 ml) Golden Cloud cake flour
1 ml salt
1 ml bicarbonate of soda
5 ml baking powder
50 ml chocolate chips
icing sugar for dusting (optional)

1 Preheat the oven to 200°C. Grease 12 cups of a standard muffin tin, greasing on top between the cups as well.
2 Beat together the butter or margarine, sugar and coffee granules, until creamy. Add the eggs and beat well. Beat in the sour cream and vanilla essence.
3 Add the flour, salt, bicarb, baking powder and chocolate chips. Mix until evenly blended; don't overmix. Divide the batter between the greased cups.
4 Place the tin into the oven, reduce the temperature to 180°C, and bake for about 20 minutes, until the muffins are golden and a cake-tester comes out clean.
5 Allow to cool in the tin for a few minutes, then loosen, lift out carefully and cool on a wire rack. Dust with icing sugar. Serve plain or with butter, or cottage or cream cheese.

> ### COOK'S NOTES
> • Replace the sour cream with plain yoghurt or buttermilk, and add 50 ml extra flour for the perfect consistency.
> • For poppy seed muffins omit the coffee and chocolate chips and add 30 ml poppy seeds.

HEALTH MUFFINS

Makes 12 extra-large muffins.

Everything a healthy heart could desire in one muffin — fruit, nuts, carrots, bran, honey and wholewheat flour.

120 g (250 ml) Golden Cloud cake flour
140 g (250 ml) Golden Cloud Krakley
    Wheat wholewheat flour
35 g (175 ml) digestive bran
20 ml baking powder
2 ml salt
100 g (250 ml) coarsely chopped pecan
    nuts, walnuts or mixed nuts
125 g (300 ml) finely chopped
    dried apricots
30 g (50 ml) seedless raisins
100 g (250 ml) coarsely grated carrots
60 ml honey or brown sugar
250 ml buttermilk
1 jumbo or 2 large eggs
75 ml sunflower or olive oil
12 whole nuts for decoration (optional)
Cinnamon Sugar (page 11)
    for sprinkling

1 Preheat the oven to 180°C. Generously grease 12 cups of a standard muffin tin, greasing on top between the cups as well.
2 Combine the flours, digestive bran, baking powder, salt, nuts, apricots, raisins, carrots and brown sugar (if using) in a bowl, and mix well to combine evenly. Make a well in the centre. Add the buttermilk, eggs, oil and honey (if using), and mix until just well combined; don't overmix.
3 Divide the batter between the muffin cups, top each with a nut and sprinkle with Cinnamon Sugar. Bake for about 20 minutes, until the muffins are golden brown and a cake-tester comes out clean.
4 Allow to cool in the tin for a few minutes, then loosen carefully and place onto a wire rack to cool completely.

CORN AND MAIZE MEAL MUFFINS

Makes 12 medium muffins

For breakfast with a South African flavour, or to serve with soup or at a braai.

200 g (400 ml) Golden Cloud cake flour
180 g (375 ml) Ace Super maize meal
30 ml sugar
2 ml bicarbonate of soda
15 ml baking powder
5 ml salt
125 g (200 ml) cooked or tinned,
    drained corn kernels
2 eggs
100 ml sunflower oil
300 ml buttermilk

1 Preheat the oven to 200°C. Generously grease 12 cups of a standard muffin tin, greasing on top between the cups.
2 Place the flour, maize meal, sugar, bicarb, baking powder, salt and corn into a mixing bowl and stir to combine evenly. Make a well in the centre.
3 Beat together the eggs, oil and buttermilk, and add to the dry ingredients. Mix until the dry ingredients are just evenly moistened; don't overmix. Divide the batter between the greased cups.
4 Place into the oven, reduce the temperature to 180°C and bake for 20 minutes, until the muffins are golden and a cake-tester comes out clean.
5 Allow to cool in the tin for a few minutes, then loosen, lift out carefully and place onto a wire rack to cool. Serve while slightly warm, with butter.

COOK'S NOTE
For a meaty variation, add about
100 ml chopped, cooked bacon or ham,
and 30–50 ml chopped spring onion and/or
chopped fresh parsley to the dry ingredients.
About 100 ml grated cheddar cheese
can be added as well.

SPICY CARROT AND MUESLI MUFFINS

Makes 12 medium muffins

*Healthy, high-fibre muffins with
spicy undertones. Delicious
with cottage cheese or slightly sweetened
creamed cottage cheese.*

300 g (600 ml) Golden Cloud cake flour
100 g (250 ml) coarsely grated carrots
125 g (250 ml) muesli
20 ml baking powder
5 ml salt
50 g (60 ml) white or brown sugar
5 ml ground cinnamon
2 ml grated nutmeg
250 ml milk
125 ml sunflower oil
2 eggs
5 ml vanilla essence
icing sugar for dusting

1 Preheat the oven to 200°C. Generously
   grease 12 cups of a standard muffin tin,
   greasing on top between the cups as well.
2 Place the flour, carrots, muesli, baking
   powder, salt, sugar, cinnamon and nutmeg
   into a mixing bowl, and stir to combine well.
   Make a well in the centre.
3 Beat together the milk, oil, eggs and vanilla
   essence, and add to the dry ingredients.
   Mix until just evenly blended. Divide the
   batter between the cups.
4 Bake for about 25 minutes, until the muffins
   are golden and a cake-tester comes out
   clean. Allow to cool in the tin for a few
   minutes, then loosen, lift out carefully and
   cool on a wire rack.

COOK'S NOTE
Although any kind of toasted muesli can be
used, the nuttier the better. If preferred,
substitute chopped pecan nuts or mixed
nuts for the muesli.

SPECKLED SAVOURY MUFFINS

Makes 12 medium muffins

180 g (375 ml) Golden Cloud cake flour
70 g (125 ml) Golden Cloud Krakley
   Wheat wholewheat flour
15 ml baking powder
10 ml sugar
2 ml salt
1–2 ml chilli powder or cayenne pepper
1–2 ml paprika
1 ml garlic and herb seasoning
125 ml finely chopped mixed red, yellow
   and green peppers
10 ml finely shredded fresh basil
50 g (125 ml) grated cheddar
   or other tasty cheese
250 ml milk
2 eggs
50 ml olive or sunflower oil
TOPPING (OPTIONAL)
50 ml finely grated cheddar or parmesan
   cheese, or a mixture of both
Red Sprinkle Mix (page 12)

1 Preheat the oven to 200°C. Grease 12 cups
   of a standard muffin tin, greasing on top
   between the cups as well.
2 Place the flours, baking powder, sugar, salt,
   chilli powder or cayenne pepper, paprika,
   garlic and herb seasoning, chopped peppers,
   basil and cheese/s into a mixing bowl, and
   mix lightly until well combined.
3 Beat together the milk, eggs and oil, and add
   to the dry ingredients. Mix until just blended;
   don't overmix. Divide between the muffin
   cups. Sprinkle lightly with the topping
   cheese and dust with Red Sprinkle Mix. Place
   into the oven, reduce the temperature
   to 180°C, and bake for about 20 minutes,
   until a cake-tester comes out clean.
4 Allow to cool in the tin for a few minutes,
   then loosen the muffins and place onto a
   wire rack to cool. Serve warm or cold.

COOK'S NOTE
Vary the flavour: add about
250 ml shredded spinach and/or sliced
mushrooms, or chopped onion. Fry everything
lightly together in a little oil before adding.

CRUMPETS

Makes about 24 crumpets, depending on size

*Make these any size you like, and serve with
butter and jam, or syrup and cream.
For thinner crumpets, add a little extra liquid
to thin the batter.*

50 g (50 ml) butter or hard margarine
240 g (500 ml) Golden Cloud cake flour
50 ml sugar (for sweet toppings), or
    30 ml sugar (for savoury toppings)
15 ml baking powder
pinch salt
2 eggs
375 ml milk
butter for frying

1 Melt the butter or margarine in a small
  saucepan, or in a jug in the microwave on
  Medium; don't make it too hot.
2 Place the flour, sugar, baking powder and salt
  into a bowl. Stir to combine. Make a well in
  the centre.
3 Beat together the eggs and milk and add to
  the dry ingredients. Mix with a whisk to form
  a smooth batter. Don't overmix. Mix in the
  melted butter or margarine. Set aside for at
  least 5 minutes.
4 Heat a little butter in a frying pan or griddle
  until moderately hot. Drop in 30–50 ml
  spoonfuls of batter; place well apart to allow
  for spreading. When nicely browned and
  bubbles appear on the surface and start to
  break, turn over with a spatula. Cook until
  golden brown on the other side. Place onto a
  wire rack and cover with a cloth to prevent
  them from drying out while you cook the
  next batches. Serve with a sweet or savoury
  filling or topping.

COOK'S NOTES
• If the batter thickens while the crumpets
are being made, add a little extra milk.
• Serve crumpets immediately, or store
in an airtight container for up to 2 days.
Reheat in an electric toaster for a few seconds.

WHOLEWHEAT CRUMPETS

Makes about 24 crumpets, depending on size

*As light as the plain variation,
but with added texture.*

50 g (50 ml) butter or hard margarine
120 g (250 ml) Golden Cloud cake flour
140 g (250 ml) Golden Cloud Krakley
    Wheat wholewheat flour
30 ml sugar
15 ml baking powder
pinch salt
2 eggs
400 ml milk
butter for frying

1 Melt the butter or margarine in a small
  saucepan, or in a jug in the microwave on
  Medium; don't make it too hot.
2 Place the flours, sugar, baking powder and
  salt into a bowl. Stir to combine. Make a
  well in the centre.
3 Beat together the eggs and milk, and add
  to the dry ingredients. Mix with a whisk to
  form a smooth batter. Don't overmix. Mix
  in the melted butter or margarine. Set aside
  for at least 5 minutes.
4 Heat a little butter in a frying pan or griddle
  until moderately hot. Drop in 30–50 ml
  spoonfuls of the batter; place well apart to
  allow for spreading. When browned, and
  bubbles appear on the surface and start to
  break, turn over with a spatula. Cook until
  golden brown on the other side. Place onto
  a wire rack and cover with a cloth to
  prevent them from drying out while you
  cook the next batches. Serve with butter, or
  a sweet or savoury filling or topping.

CRUMPET STACK WITH
CARAMEL CREAM CHEESE

Makes 6 stacks of 3 crumpets, or 9 stacks of 2

*Plain or wholewheat crumpets stacked and
filled with a delicious sweet-cheesy filling.*

18 cooked Crumpets (Plain or
    Wholewheat)
fresh fruit: banana, berries or kiwifruit
chopped nuts or toasted muesli
icing sugar for dusting
CARAMEL CREAM CHEESE
50 ml honey or syrup
50 ml brown sugar
15 ml butter or hard margarine
30 ml water
2 ml vanilla essence
15 ml cornflour
50 ml water
250 g cottage cheese

1 To make the caramel cream cheese filling,
  place the honey or syrup, sugar, butter or
  margarine, water and vanilla essence into
  a medium saucepan. Heat slowly, stirring
  ocassionally, until melted. Or place into a jug
  and microwave on Medium for about
  2 minutes, stirring ocassionally, until melted.
2 Mix the cornflour with the water and add
  to the hot mixture. Bring to the boil, stirring
  continuously until smooth and thick.
  Simmer for 3 minutes. To cook in the
  microwave: add the cornflour and water to
  the hot mixture and microwave on Medium
  for 2 minutes until thickened. Beat well.
3 Cool the topping to room temperature, then
  beat in the cottage cheese with a whisk,
  until evenly combined.
4 Stack the crumpets in layers of 2 or 3 with
  caramel cream cheese, and fruit, nuts or
  muesli in between. Dust with icing sugar.

COOK'S NOTE
Caramel cream cheese can be refrigerated
in a sealed container for up to a week.

MUESLI CRUMPETS WITH FRUIT

Makes about 24 crumpets, depending on size

Crumpets make a fabulously healthy breakfast, especially when they're made with muesli and topped with yoghurt and fruit.

240 g (500 ml) Golden Cloud cake flour
50 ml sugar
15 ml baking powder
pinch salt
2 eggs
375 ml milk
50 g (50 ml) butter or hard margarine
100 g (250 ml) toasted muesli
   (approximate amount)
butter for frying
TO SERVE
plain yoghurt or whipped cream
fresh fruit
honey or syrup

1 Combine the flour, sugar, baking powder and salt in a bowl. Make a well in the centre.
2 Beat together the eggs and milk. Add to the dry ingredients. Mix with a whisk to a smooth batter; don't overmix.
3 Melt the butter or margarine in a small saucepan, or in a jug in the microwave on Medium; don't make it too hot. Mix into the batter. Set aside for at least 5 minutes.
4 Heat a little butter in a frying pan or griddle until moderately hot. Drop in 30–50 ml spoonfuls of the batter; place well apart to allow for spreading. Place a spoonful of muesli in the centre of each crumpet. When golden brown and bubbles appear on the surface and start to break, turn over with a spatula. Cook until golden brown on the other side.
5 Place the crumpets onto a wire rack and cover with a cloth to prevent them from drying out while you prepare the next batches.
6 To serve, stack 2–3 crumpets on each plate. Stack with fruit and yoghurt or cream, and drizzle with honey or syrup.

BUTTERMILK FLAPJACKS

Makes 12–16 flapjacks, depending on size

Flapjacks, also known as griddle cakes, are thick, tender and light. Serve with cinnamon sugar, jam or syrup and cream, or turn them into a wonderful American-style breakfast with maple syrup and bacon, ham or sausage on the side. They're also delicious with grated cheese, or cottage or cream cheese. To make small flapjacks, thin the batter with a little water.

60 g (60 ml) butter or hard margarine
3 eggs
500 ml buttermilk
240 g (500 ml) Golden Cloud cake flour
5 ml bicarbonate of soda
pinch salt
15 ml sugar
butter for frying

1 Melt the butter or margarine in a small saucepan, or in a jug in the microwave on Medium; don't make it too hot.
2 Separate the eggs. Beat together the egg yolks and buttermilk. Place the flour, bicarb, salt and sugar into a mixing bowl, and make a well in the centre. Add the egg mixture and beat with a whisk to a smooth batter; don't overmix. Stir in the melted butter or margarine.
3 Beat the egg whites until stiff, and fold into the batter until evenly combined. Set aside for at least 5 minutes.
4 Heat a little butter in a frying pan or griddle until moderately hot. Drop in 80 ml spoonfuls of the batter; place well apart to allow for spreading. When nicely browned and bubbles appear on the surface and start to break, turn over with a spatula. Cook until golden brown on the other side, and firm when pressed.
5 Place the flapjacks on a wire rack and cover with a cloth to prevent them from drying out while preparing the next batches. Serve while still slightly warm, or cool.

VARIATIONS
SAVOURY & SWEET FILLED
FLAPJACKS OR CRUMPETS

Spoon about 50 ml of any of these fillings onto each flapjack or crumpet, as the batter begins to set. Cover with a thin layer of batter, allow to set slightly, then flip and cook until golden on the other side. Serve the savoury flapjacks with salad as a light meal. Serve sweet flapjacks or crumpets as a dessert or tea-time treat.

Bacon and Cheese Filling
Mix together 250 g cooked and coarsely chopped bacon or shredded ham, 200 g grated cheddar cheese, and 50 ml each chopped fresh parsley and chopped spring onion.

Ham and Corn Filling
Mix together 250 g finely shredded ham, 250 ml cream-style sweetcorn, 250 ml whole kernel corn, and 50 ml each chopped fresh parsley and spring onion. Serve with grated cheddar cheese.

Chicken and Mushroom Filling
Mix together 250 g finely shredded cooked chicken, 250 g sliced mushrooms, 125 ml bean sprouts, and 50 ml chopped spring onion. Heat 30 ml butter or margarine in a frying pan and stir-fry the ingredients until crisp-tender. Season with salt and milled black pepper.

Banana and Pecan Filling
Scatter each flapjack or crumpet with a few thin slices of banana and coarsely chopped pecan nuts. Serve with maple syrup and whipped cream or ice cream, and a dusting of Cinnamon Sugar (page 11).

Apple and Cinnamon Filling
Mix together a 410 g tin of pie apples, coarsely chopped, 10 ml ground cinnamon and 30 ml sugar. Spoon about 30 ml of this mixture onto each flapjack or crumpet. Serve with syrup and whipped cream or cream cheese and Cinnamon Sugar (page 11).

Chocolate-chip Filling
250 g chocolate chips. Place 15 ml onto each flapjack or crumpet. Serve with whipped cream and syrup.

PANCAKES

Makes 8–10 pancakes

Pancakes are thinner and lighter than crumpets and flapjacks. Roll, stack or fold them into triangles or parcels filled with a sprinkling of cinnamon sugar and topped with a squeeze of lemon juice or syrup. Or fill with a savoury filling.

250 ml milk
1 egg
15 ml sunflower oil
120 g (250 ml) Golden Cloud cake flour
5 ml baking powder
1 ml salt
100 ml water (approximate amount)
sunflower oil for frying

1 Mix together the milk, egg and oil in a jug. Place the flour, baking powder and salt into a mixing bowl, and make a well in the centre.
2 Add about two-thirds of the milk mixture, and blend with a whisk to a smooth, thick batter. Gradually add the remaining milk mixture and sufficient of the water until the batter has the consistency of thick pouring cream. Mix only until blended. Alternatively, place all the ingredients into the bowl of a food processor or liquidiser and blend for 1 minute only. Overmixing will toughen the pancakes. If time allows, let the batter rest for 30–60 minutes. Stir gently but thoroughly before cooking.
3 Pour a few drops of oil into a pancake pan, spread over the base and heat well. Pour in about 75 ml batter (depending on the size of the pan) and tilt the pan to cover the base evenly. Cook until bubbles appear and the batter starts to set. Shake the pan to ensure the pancake isn't sticking, and cook until golden.
4 Toss or turn the pancake with a spatula, and cook until golden on the other side. Serve straight from the pan or keep warm in the oven, or in a covered dish placed over simmering water.

COOK'S NOTES

• A pancake pan measures 15–22 cm in diameter and has shallow, sloping sides so that you can easily slide in a spatula to flip the pancake. It should be comfortable and light to handle, with a smooth surface that will not stick, and a flat, even base that will heat up quickly and evenly on the stovetop.
• Pancakes that are cooked too slowly are pale and tough, so start cooking over high heat, then reduce the heat. Electric pancake makers work well, provided the instructions are carried out correctly.
• Oil in the batter minimizes greasing of the pan during cooking.
• The side that is cooked first looks best; serve with this side on the outside.
• Cool cooked pancakes before stacking if you are serving them later. Wrap in clingfilm and refrigerate for a day or two, or freeze. Thaw and reheat a few pancakes at a time in the microwave on Medium (about 20 seconds per pancake).

CHEESE BLINTZES

Makes 8 average blintzes

Pancake batter (page 39)
sunflower oil for frying
CHEESE FILLING
500 g firm cottage or cream cheese
2 egg yolks
2 ml vanilla essence
2 ml lemon juice
10 ml sugar
FOR FRYING BLINTZES
50 g (50 ml) butter or hard margarine
50 ml sunflower oil
TO SERVE
250 ml cream
Cinnamon Sugar (page 11)

1 Prepare the pancake batter. Heat a few drops of oil in a 20 cm pancake pan. Spoon in enough batter to coat the base of the pan evenly, tilting it from side to side.
2 Cover partly with a lid and cook over moderate heat until golden underneath and set and dry on top. Don't turn the pancake over; cook on one side only. Turn out onto a greased plate. Continue cooking, until all the pancakes are done.
3 Combine the cream cheese or cottage cheese, egg yolks, vanilla essence, lemon juice and sugar in a bowl, and stir gently without softening the cheese. Divide the filling between the pancakes, using about 60 ml for each. Fold over about 40 mm from each side, then the top and bottom edges to form a parcel. Place seam down onto a greased plate. Cover and refrigerate.
4 Shortly before serving, heat the butter or margarine and oil in a large frying pan. Fry the blintzes carefully, seam-side down first, until golden and crisp on both sides.
5 Serve as soon as possible. If kept warm for more than 5 minutes, the texture of the filling will be spoilt.
6 Place the warm blintzes onto plates, spoon whipped cream on top and sprinkle with Cinnamon Sugar (page 11).

COOK'S NOTES
• Filled Cheese Blintzes can be kept refrigerated for up to a day before frying.
• This recipe requires last minute attention, which makes it difficult to serve to more than 8 people simultaneously. To speed up the cooking process, use two frying pans, or bake them in the oven. Arrange the blintzes in a greased ovenproof dish, dot each with 10 ml butter or margarine, and bake at 200°C for 15 minutes, until crisp.
• To make Smoked Salmon Blintzes, mix together 250 g finely chopped smoked salmon, 250 g firm cottage cheese, 5 ml chopped fresh dill or 1 ml dried dill, 5 ml lemon juice, 250 ml sour cream and milled black pepper. Spoon 50 ml of filling into each blintz.

COOK'S NOTE
For the Apple Blintzes, use a 410 g tin of pie apples instead of fresh apples. Place half the tin of apples into a saucepan and follow the method as described.

APPLE BLINTZES

Makes 8 average blintzes

Fruit-filled blintzes make a mouth-watering dessert.

Pancake batter (page 39)
sunflower oil for frying
APPLE FILLING
4 large cooking apples
60 ml water
5 ml lemon juice
2 ml ground cinnamon
1 ml mixed spice
30 ml sugar
15 ml cornflour
15 ml chopped pecan nuts, or walnuts
15 ml seedless raisins (optional)

1 Prepare and cook the pancakes as described for Cheese Blintzes.
2 To make the filling, peel and slice 2 of the apples and place into a medium saucepan with half the water, and the lemon juice, spices and sugar. Cook until quite soft. Mash with a fork. Peel and coarsely chop the remaining apples and add to the purée. Simmer, uncovered, for 2 minutes.
3 Mix the cornflour with the remaining water, and stir into the pan. Add the nuts and raisins (if using), and simmer until thickened. Allow to cool.
4 Divide the filling between the pancakes, using approximately 60 ml for each. Fold over about 40 mm from each side, then the top and bottom edges to enclose the filling completely and make parcels. Place seam down onto greased plates. Cover and refrigerate.
5 Shortly before serving, heat the butter or margarine and oil in a large shallow frying pan, and place the blintzes into the pan, seam-side down first. Fry carefully until golden and crisp on both sides.
6 Place the blintzes onto a platter and serve immediately.

WAFFLES

Mix the batter gently yet quickly for crisp, tender waffles. Don't beat or overmix or the waffles will be tough.

100 g (100 ml) butter or hard margarine
240 g (500 ml) Golden Cloud cake flour
10 ml baking powder
2 ml salt
20 ml sugar (sweet waffles),
  or 5 ml sugar (savoury waffles)
3 eggs
400 ml milk

1 Melt the butter or margarine in a small saucepan, or in a jug in the microwave on Medium; don't make it too hot. Combine the flour, baking powder, salt and sugar in a mixing bowl. Make a well in the centre.
2 Separate the eggs. Beat together the yolks and milk and pour into the dry ingredients, together with the melted butter or margarine. Using a large whisk, mix together with a few swift strokes until just moistened – the batter need not be completely smooth.
3 Beat the egg whites until stiff. Fold into the batter until barely blended.
4 Heat the waffle iron until the light indicates that it is ready. Using a soup ladle, pour and spread sufficient batter onto the bottom plate to cover about two-thirds of the surface. Adjust the amount of batter until the waffles shape perfectly.
5 Close the waffle iron and cook for 2–3 minutes. When steam no longer escapes from the sides and the waffle iron opens easily, the waffle should be ready. If not, leave a while longer, until it's puffed, crisp and golden. Remove the waffle with a blunt instrument to prevent scratching the surface of the plates. Trim the edges if necessary.
6 Place the waffle on a plate, top with sweet (syrup, honey, chocolate sauce, cream or ice cream) or savoury (cheese and savoury sauces) toppings, and serve immediately.

BUTTERMILK WAFFLES

Makes 6–8 waffles, depending on size

Prepare and cook these flavourful crisp waffles according to the method described alongside, but with the ingredients given below.

100 g (100 ml) butter or hard margarine
240 g (500 ml) Golden Cloud cake flour
1 ml bicarbonate of soda
7 ml baking powder
15 ml sugar
3 ml salt
2 eggs
500 ml buttermilk

COOK'S NOTES
• The batter needs to be the correct consistency to prevent leaking and allow for even spreading in the waffle iron. If it contains enough butter or margarine it shouldn't stick to a well-heated iron. If it sticks, lightly brush the clean iron with oil before cooking the waffles.
• The batter can stand at room temperature for a while or in the fridge for several hours. To serve 6–8 waffles simultaneously, place freshly cooked waffles in single layers onto the shelves of the oven set at 100°C.

WAFFLE VARIATIONS
Banana Waffles
Add 250 ml thinly sliced ripe banana to the batter before folding in the egg white. Serve with cream, syrup and cinnamon sugar.
Pecan Nut Waffles
Add 125 ml chopped nuts to the batter and top with ice cream or cream, and maple syrup.
Chocolate-chip Waffles
Add 125 ml chocolate chips to the basic batter and top generously with cream and syrup, hot chocolate sauce or fruit sauce.
Cheese Waffles
Substitute 125 ml finely grated, well-flavoured cheese, and 50 ml melted butter or margarine for the 100 ml melted butter or margarine in the basic recipe. Serve with a little extra grated cheese, grilled bacon and tomato.

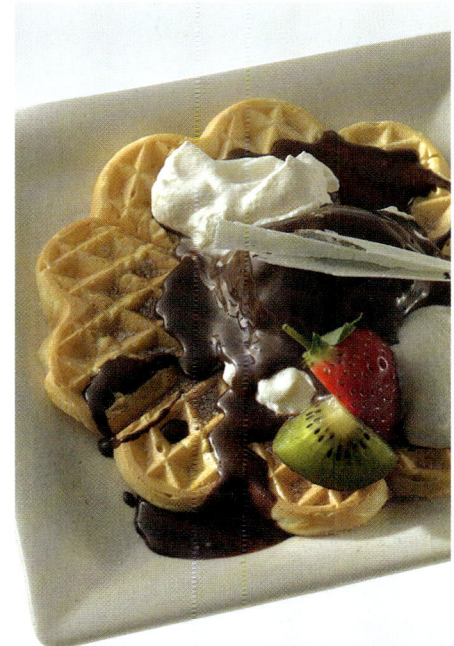

QUICK CAKES & LOAVES

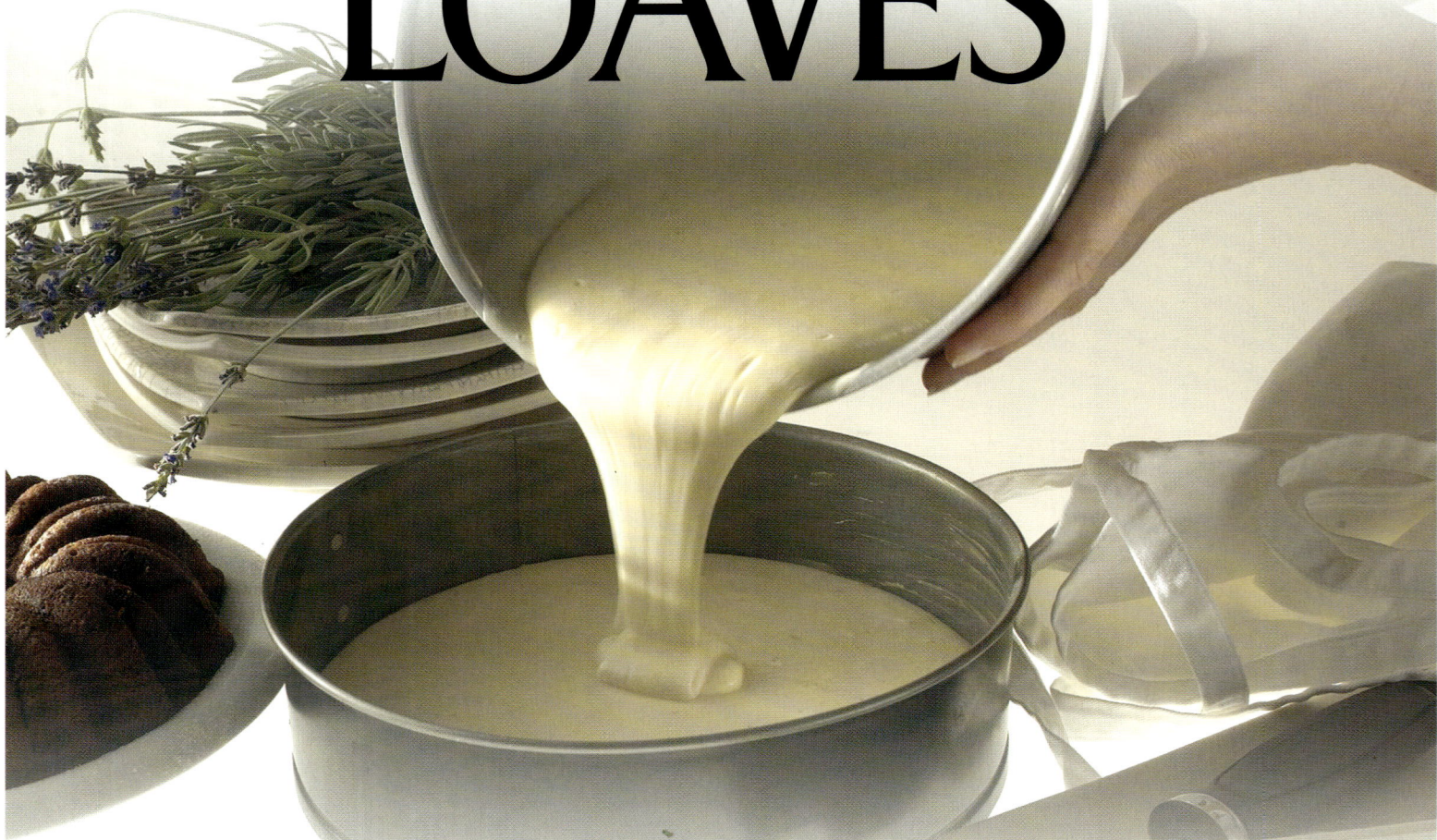

Many aspiring bakers are daunted by the thought of baking a cake. But there's really no mystery involved. All you need to do is to measure, mix, turn the mixture into the prepared tin, and pop it into the oven. And with food processors and electric mixers, cake-baking is certainly not as difficult for us as it was for our mothers and grandmothers.

There are, however, a few golden rules: all ingredients should be measured correctly (more accurately than when making a stew, for example); the baking tin should be of the correct dimensions; and the oven should be preset to exactly the prescribed temperature.

If you don't have the time or inclination to conjure up an intricately iced, perfectly garnished cake, this is the chapter for you. It's filled with cakes and sweet loaves that are quick to mix and quite happy to be served plain. Of course, if you wish to pretty them up a bit, add a dusting of icing sugar, or place flowers alongside the cake or loaf.

Many of the cakes and loaves in this section last well for several days, making them perfect for snacks, teas, or lunchbox treats. Some are good for freezing; make sure, though, that they're packed in airtight containers, and thaw completely before freshening up for a few minutes in the oven.

German Stollen page 48

Spicy Apple Ring Cake page 52

Custard Cake page 50

GINGER SPONGE LOAF

Serves 10–12

This loaf has a marvellous moist texture and a rich, spicy flavour. For an irresistible dessert serve the loaf sliced, with custard or cream and poached or canned pears.

120 g (250 ml) Golden Cloud cake flour
10 ml ground ginger
5 ml ground cinnamon
2 ml ground cloves
2 ml grated nutmeg
10 ml baking powder
2 ml bicarbonate of soda
generous pinch salt
80 g (100 ml) sugar
100 ml golden syrup or maple syrup
100 ml sunflower oil
100 ml water
5 ml vanilla essence
3 eggs

1 Preheat the oven to 180°C. Line a medium (26 cm) loaf tin with nonstick baking paper or waxed paper. Allow the long sides to extend slightly over the edges of the tin. If using waxed paper, grease the paper as well as the short sides of the tin.
2 Combine the flour, ginger, cinnamon, cloves, nutmeg, baking powder, bicarb, salt and sugar in a bowl. Add the syrup, oil, water and vanilla essence. Beat until just smooth.
3 Separate the eggs and beat the yolks into the batter. In another bowl, beat the egg whites until firm. Fold into the batter until evenly combined. Pour into the prepared tin and bake for 35–40 minutes until the loaf is well risen and firm to the touch, and a cake-tester comes out clean.
4 Switch off the oven, open the door and allow the loaf to cool in the oven for 5 minutes. Remove from the oven and allow to cool in the tin for 5 minutes more. Turn out, peel off the paper and place on a plate. Slice and serve as is, or lightly buttered.

STREUSEL BUTTER CAKE

Serves 12–16

100 g (100 ml) butter or hard margarine, softened
150 g (200 ml) sugar
180 g (375 ml) Golden Cloud cake flour
10 ml baking powder
pinch salt
1 egg
150 ml milk
5 ml vanilla essence and/or 10 ml finely grated lemon zest

STREUSEL TOPPING
50 g (75 ml) sugar
10 ml ground cinnamon
100 g (250 ml) pecans or walnuts

1 Preheat the oven to 180°C. Generously grease a small baking dish (30 x 20 cm).
2 Place all the ingredients for the cake into a food processor or into the bowl of an electric mixer. Blend for 2 minutes or beat for 4–5 minutes to a smooth batter. Spoon the batter into the dish and spread evenly. Make the centre slightly hollow to compensate for rising while baking.
3 Mix the topping ingredients and sprinkle evenly onto the batter, pressing it in very lightly. Bake for about 30 minutes until the cake is firm and golden brown. Cut into neat squares and serve from the dish, slightly warm or cooled. The cake keeps well for up to 2 days.

OLIVE OIL CAKE

Serves 10–20

Olive oil increases the cost in this simple yet delicious cake, but it decreases the amount of saturated fat in the recipe.

280 g (500 ml) Golden Cloud
    self-raising flour
200 g (250 ml) sugar
pinch salt
200 ml light olive oil
3 eggs
150 ml milk
2 ml vanilla essence
icing sugar for dusting
Sweetened Whipped Cream (page 80)
    for serving (optional)
FLAVOURING INGREDIENTS: choose from
10 ml caraway seed or aniseed
10 ml finely grated orange or lemon
    zest, plus 15 ml juice
125 ml chocolate chips
2 ml almond essence, plus 50 g flaked
    almonds to sprinkle in the greased tin
    and on top of the cake before baking

1 Preheat the oven to 180°C. Generously grease a 22 cm fluted or 25 cm deep-ring pan. If using flaked almonds, sprinkle half evenly into the tin.
2 Place the flour, sugar, salt, olive oil, eggs, milk and vanilla essence into a mixing bowl or the bowl of a food processor. Beat or process until smooth. Add the flavouring ingredient of your choice, and mix or process on pulse until just combined.
3 Pour the batter into the prepared tin and smooth the top. Sprinkle the remaining almonds on top, if used. Bake for about 30 minutes, until the cake is golden and firm to the touch and a cake-tester comes out clean.
4 Turn the cake out carefully onto a wire rack, and allow to cool completely. Place or a plate and dust with icing sugar. If you like, serve with whipped cream.

WHOLEWHEAT DATE GINGERBREAD

Serves 12–16

100 g (175 ml) stoned dates,
    finely chopped
100 g (100 ml) butter or hard margarine
100 g (125 ml) brown sugar
125 ml golden syrup or maple syrup
250 g (400 ml) Golden Cloud Krakley
    Wheat wholewheat flour
7 ml bicarbonate of soda
2 ml ground cloves
20 ml ground ginger
5 ml mixed spice
1 ml salt
100 ml milk
2 eggs
50 g (125 ml) chopped pecan nuts
    (optional)

1 Preheat the oven to180°C. Grease one
  medium (26 cm) loaf tin.
2 Place the dates, butter or margarine, brown
  sugar and syrup into a jug. Microwave on
  Medium until the butter or margarine has
  melted; don't make it too hot. Alternatively
  place the ingredients in a small saucepan
  and heat until melted. Mash lightly with a
  fork to soften the dates. Allow to cool.
3 Place the flour, bicarb, cloves, ginger, mixed
  spice and salt into a mixing bowl, and stir to
  combine. Make a well in the centre. Add the
  cooled date mixture, as well as the milk, eggs
  and nuts (if used), and beat to make a
  smooth batter.
4 Pour into the tin. Bake for about 45 minutes,
  until a cake-tester comes out clean. Allow
  to cool in the tin for a few minutes, then
  loosen and turn out onto a wire rack to
  cool completely.

BANANA GINGERBREAD LOAF

Serves 12–16

Two old favourites combined.

6 very ripe bananas, peeled
4 eggs
200 g (250 ml) brown sugar
200 g (225 ml) butter or hard
    margarine, softened
100 ml milk
30 ml golden syrup or honey
5 ml vanilla essence
250 g (500 ml) Golden Cloud cake flour
20 ml ground ginger
5 ml ground cinnamon
5 ml mixed spice
12 ml baking powder
2 ml bicarbonate of soda
1 ml salt

1 Preheat the oven to 180°C. Generously
  grease one large (28 cm) loaf tin.
2 Place the bananas, eggs, brown sugar, butter
  or margarine, milk, syrup or honey, and
  vanilla essence into a food processor and
  blend for about 1 minute until smooth. If
  using an electric mixer, mash the bananas
  and place them into a bowl with the eggs,
  brown sugar, butter or margarine, milk,
  syrup or honey, and vanilla essence. Beat
  until well combined.
3 Add the flour, ginger, cinnamon, mixed spice,
  baking powder, bicarb and salt, and process
  for a few seconds until blended, or beat to a
  smooth batter. Pour into the prepared tin.
4 Place in the oven and reduce the temperature
  to 160°C. Bake for about 50 minutes, until the
  loaf is firm to the touch and a cake-tester
  comes out clean. If the top browns too much
  or too soon, reduce the temperature to 150°C.
5 Allow the loaf to cool in the tin for
  5 minutes. Loosen the sides and shake the
  tin to release the loaf. Turn out onto a wire
  rack, and allow to cool completely. Serve
  sliced and buttered.

BUTTERMILK BANANA LOAF

Serves 10–12

2 eggs
150 g (200 ml) sugar
3–4 (depending on size) very ripe
   bananas, peeled
125 ml buttermilk
15 ml sunflower oil
15 ml vanilla essence
250 g (500 ml) Golden Cloud cake flour
10 ml baking powder
2 ml bicarbonate of soda
2 ml salt
50 g (125 ml) pecans or walnuts (optional)
Cinnamon Sugar, page 11 (optional)
a few additional halved nuts (optional)

1 Preheat the oven to 160°C. Generously grease one medium (26 cm) loaf tin.
2 Place the eggs, sugar, bananas, buttermilk, oil, vanilla essence, flour, baking powder, bicarb and salt into the bowl of a food processor and process for 1 minute to a smooth batter; don't overprocess. Add the nuts and pulse 3–4 times to mix them into the batter without chopping them too finely. To make by hand, beat together the eggs and sugar until pale and creamy. Mash the bananas very well with a fork and add to the bowl with the buttermilk, oil, vanilla essence, flour, baking powder, bicarb and salt. Chop the nuts and add to the batter.
3 Pour the batter into the prepared tin, smooth the top and sprinkle lightly with cinnamon sugar if you wish. Decorate with halved nuts.
4 Bake for about 45 minutes, until the loaf is firm to the touch and a cake-tester comes out clean. Allow to cool in the tin for a few minutes. Shake and turn out onto a wire rack.

COOK'S NOTES
• To ensure a moist, sweet loaf, bananas must be very ripe or slightly past their prime.
• For a slightly nuttier cake substitute half the cake flour with wholewheat flour.
• To enrich this healthy loaf with fibre, add a small quantity (30 ml) raisins and/or sultanas, or a spoonful or two of wheat germ or digestive bran, to the batter.
• If you wish, replace the buttermilk with plain yoghurt.

GERMAN STOLLEN

This fruity, country-style cake is a traditional Christmas treat. This quick version is made with baking powder instead of yeast, so it's easy to make.

FRUIT COMBINATION
125 g (200 ml) seedless raisins
125 g (200 ml) bleached sultanas
50 g (75 ml) currants or additional
    raisins
100 g red glacé cherries
100 g green glacé cherries or mixed peel
CAKE
250 ml brandy or rum
150 g (175 ml) butter or hard
    margarine, softened
200 g (250 ml) sugar
2 eggs
250 g (250 ml) creamed cottage cheese
2 ml almond essence
15 ml lemon juice or 1 ml lemon essence
500 g (1 litre) Golden Cloud cake flour
2 ml salt
15 ml baking powder
100 g (250 ml) slivered almonds, roasted
    in a dry frying pan
200 g marzipan (optional)
150 g (175 ml) melted butter or
    margarine for brushing onto loaves
icing sugar for dusting

1 Grease one large or two small baking trays, depending on how many cakes you plan to make. Place all the fruit into a bowl, pour over the brandy or rum, and set aside for at least 1 hour to soften and flavour the fruit. Preheat the oven to 190°C.
2 Place the butter or margarine and sugar into a mixing bowl, and beat well by hand or with an electric mixer until pale and creamy. Add the eggs, cottage cheese, almond essence and lemon juice or essence and beat well. Add half the flour, together with the salt and baking powder, and mix until evenly blended.

3 Drain the fruit and add to the cake mixture with the nuts. Mix lightly to combine. Add the remaining flour and mix lightly to make a soft dough. Mix and knead very gently until smooth.
4 Divide the dough into two. Roll out separately into ovals about 25 mm thick on a lightly floured surface, with a floured rolling pin. If using marzipan, roll it into sausage shapes and place down the centre of each oval of dough. Fold over neatly and place on the baking tray/s.
5 Place the baking tray/s into the oven, reduce the temperature to 180°C and bake for about 40 minutes until the stollen are golden and firm, and a cake-tester comes out clean.
6 Lift onto a wire rack and brush repeatedly with the melted butter or margarine, until it is completely absorbed. Dust generously with icing sugar. Cool completely. Serve sliced and buttered, or store in an airtight container.

COOK'S NOTES
• The recipe calls for 500 g dried fruit, which can be made up in different ways according to preference and availability. If you wish, substitute the fruit with 500 g fruit cake mix. If you prefer a less fruity loaf, reduce the amount of fruit to 300 g.
• If preferred, bake three or four small stollens, and reduce the baking time accordingly. The baked cakes freeze very well.
• Thaw and reheat slightly at 160°C for the best results.

SOUR CREAM LOAF WITH CARDAMOM & PISTACHIOS

Serves 12-16

Intriguing, lingering flavours ...

100 g (100 ml) butter or hard
    margarine, softened
200 g (250 ml) sugar
4 eggs
5 ml vanilla essence
pinch salt (if salted nuts are used) or
    1 ml salt (if unsalted nuts are used)
5 ml bicarbonate of soda
5 ml ground cardamom
1 ml ground cinnamon
250 g (500 ml) Golden Cloud cake flour
250 ml sour cream
100 g (250 ml) shelled and coarsely
    chopped or halved pistachio nuts

TOPPING
30 ml sugar
1 ml ground cardamom
1 ml ground cinnamon

1 Preheat the oven to 180°C. Generously grease a medium (26 cm) loaf tin.
2 Place the butter or margarine and sugar into a mixing bowl, or the bowl of an electric mixer, and beat well until creamed. Add the eggs one by one, beating constantly. Beat in the vanilla essence.
3 Add the salt, bicarb, cardamom, cinnamon and half the flour, and beat to combine. Beat in the sour cream. Add the remaining flour and nuts and mix until evenly combined.
4 Spoon the batter into the greased tin and smooth the top. Make the centre area slightly hollow to compensate for rising while baking.
5 Combine the ingredients for the topping and sprinkle onto the surface. Bake for about 40 minutes, until the loaf is firm to the touch and a cake-tester comes out clean.
6 Allow to cool in the tin for 5 minutes, then loosen carefully and turn out onto a plate. Slice and serve immediately.

COOK'S NOTES
• Use unsalted roasted nuts if possible, or shell the salted roasted nuts and rub them between your palms to remove excess salt. Adjust the salt in the recipe as explained.
• The cake freezes very well when sealed in an airtight container or wrapped in foil. Thaw for about 2 hours at room temperature.
• Or, store in an airtight container for 2–3 days after you have allowed the cake to cool completely.
• For two smaller loaves, bake in two smaller tins. Reduce the baking time to approximately 30 minutes.

VARIATIONS
Use the same basic recipe and replace the spices and pistachios with the following ingredients:

Lemon Loaf
Add 30 ml lemon juice and 15 ml finely grated lemon zest to the mixture.
Almond Loaf
Add 2 ml almond essence and 100 g (250 ml) lightly roasted flaked almonds, or half almonds, half sultanas, to the mixture.
Cherry Loaf
Add 100 g (150 ml) whole red glacé cherries to the mixture.

CUSTARD CAKE

Serves 8–10

Enjoy this creamy custard baked into layers of crisp, custard-flavoured butter cake as is, or serve it for dessert with sweetened whipped cream and fresh berries or drained tinned gooseberries or cherries.

CUSTARD FILLING
15 ml custard powder
30 ml cornflour
30 ml sugar
small pinch salt
350 ml milk
15 ml butter or hard margarine
5 ml vanilla essence

CAKE
100 g (100 ml) butter or hard
   margarine, softened
125 g (150 ml) castor sugar
2 eggs
5 ml vanilla essence
120 g (250 ml) Golden Cloud cake flour
5 ml baking powder
15 ml custard powder
generous pinch salt
icing sugar for dusting

1 Preheat the oven to 180°C. Generously grease a 22 cm springform tin.
2 To cook the custard in the microwave oven (on High throughout), place the custard powder, cornflour, sugar, salt and milk into a large (2 litre) microwave-safe jug, and beat well with a whisk. Microwave for 90 seconds. Beat well. Microwave for a further 90 seconds, until thickened. Beat in the butter or margarine and vanilla essence. Microwave for 30 seconds, then beat well. To cook on the stovetop, place the custard powder, cornflour, sugar, salt and milk into a saucepan, and beat well with a whisk. Bring to the boil over moderate heat, beating until smooth and thick. Remove from heat and beat in the butter or margarine and vanilla essence. Allow to cool, beating from time to time to prevent a skin from forming. To cool quickly, place the jug or saucepan into a basin of iced water.
3 To make the cake, place all the ingredients into the bowl of a food processor and whizz for 1 minute until smooth. If using in an electric mixer, beat together the butter or margarine and castor sugar until smooth and well creamed. Beat in the eggs and vanilla essence. Add the flour, baking powder, custard powder and salt. Beat until well mixed.
4 Spoon a little more than half the batter into the prepared tin. Spread evenly onto the base and about 4 cm up the sides. Drop spoonfuls – slightly apart – of the cooled custard onto the batter. Smooth gently with the back of a spoon.
5 Place spoonfuls of the remaining batter onto the custard, and spread carefully and evenly to cover the custard completely. Scrape down the batter on the sides of the cake tin over the custard to cover it at the edges. Don't worry if it's a little uneven; the cake will still look great.
6 Bake for about 30 minutes until the cake is golden and firm to the touch. Switch off the oven, open the door, and allow the cake to cool in the oven for 10 minutes. Remove from the oven and cool, in the tin, for a further 20 minutes until the custard is set.
7 Remove the cooled cake from the base of tin using a large spatula, and place it onto a plate. Dust with icing sugar.

> **COOK'S NOTES**
> • This cake will break if you attempt to lift it from the base of the tin while it's still hot.
> • If you wish to serve it as a warm dessert, bake it in a 22 cm pie dish and serve directly from the dish.

DATE AND NUT LOAF

Serves 12–16

250 g (400 ml) stoned dates,
   finely chopped
5 ml bicarbonate of soda
80 g (100 ml) caramel sugar
80 g (100 ml) white sugar
100 g (100 ml) butter or hard
   margarine
5 ml vanilla essence
300 ml boiling water, or 250 ml boiling
   water plus 50 ml brandy
300 g (625 ml) Golden Cloud cake flour
5 ml baking powder
2 ml salt
a pinch each of ground cinnamon,
   mixed spice and ground ginger
   (optional)
50–100 g (125–250 ml) coarsely
   chopped pecans, walnuts or unsalted
   mixed nuts
1 egg

1 Preheat the oven to 180°C. Generously grease a medium (26 cm) loaf tin.
2. Place the dates, bicarb, sugars, butter or margarine and vanilla essence into a bowl and pour over the boiling water or the boiling water and brandy. Stir to combine. Set aside for about 5 minutes to cool. Stir and mash lightly with a fork to break up the dates.
3 Place the flour, baking powder, salt and spices (if used) into a mixing bowl, and add the cooled date mixture, nuts and egg. Mix well to combine evenly.
4 Spoon the batter into the tin and smooth the top. Bake for about 45 minutes until the loaf is firm to the touch, and a cake-tester comes out clean.
5 Allow the loaf to cool in the tin for about 5 minutes before turning out onto a wire rack. Turn over, cool a while longer and serve while still slightly warm, sliced and buttered – with the butter melting into the slices! Or allow to cool completely and store in an airtight container.

MANGO CAKE

Serves 12–16

A special treat crammed with the rich, tropical flavour of ripe mangoes. A must-have recipe when mangoes are in season.

4 eggs
125 g (150 ml) castor sugar
250 g (280 ml) butter or hard margarine, softened
125 g (150 ml) castor sugar
5 ml vanilla essence
280 ml mango purée (1 large or 2 small, ripe mangoes)
250 g (500 ml) Golden Cloud cake flour
10 ml baking powder
5 ml ground cinnamon
50 g (125 ml) chopped pecan nuts
2 ml salt

ICING
50 g (50 ml) butter or hard margarine, softened
130 g (250 ml) icing sugar
5 ml lemon juice
chopped pecan nuts to decorate

1 Preheat the oven to 170°C. Generously grease a 25 cm deep-ring tin.
2 Separate the eggs; set the yolks aside. Beat the egg whites until stiff. Beat in the first measure of castor sugar gradually to make a stiff meringue.
3 Cream the butter or margarine and second measure of castor sugar very well in a food processor or with an electric mixer. Add the egg yolks, vanilla essence and 250 ml of the mango purée. Beat well.
4 Add the flour, baking powder, cinnamon, pecans and salt, and mix until combined.

Fold in the egg white. Pour into the prepared tin. Bake for 50–60 minutes, until the cake is firm and a cake-tester comes out clean. Allow to cool in the tin for 10 minutes, then turn out onto a wire rack to cool completely.
5 To make the icing, beat together the butter or margarine, icing sugar, lemon juice and the remaining mango purée until smooth in a food processor or with an electric mixer. Add a little extra icing sugar if necessary. Spread onto the cake and sprinkle with nuts.

COOK'S NOTES
• If you're using tinned mangoes, drain well and reduce the first measure of castor sugar to 75 g (100 ml).
• For a coarsely textured cake, add extra nuts.
• For a more practical storage shape, bake in two small loaf tins.
• Refrigerate in an airtight container.

SPICY APPLE RING CAKE

Serves 10-12

Light as a feather, the flavour improves if this cake is kept in an airtight container for a day or two. Bake in a cake or loaf tin, and serve plain or add the topping to make it fancy and rich. If you use the topping, refrigerate. The cake also freezes very well.

2 eggs
150 g (200 ml) sugar
250 ml sunflower oil
200 ml apple sauce
200 g (400 ml) Golden Cloud cake flour
5 ml ground cinnamon
2 ml mixed spice
1 ml ground cloves
1 ml grated nutmeg
1 ml salt
5 ml bicarbonate of soda
30 ml brandy, rum or sherry (optional)
TOPPING (optional for fluted cake)
½ x 380 g tin caramel
50 ml chopped pecan nuts or walnuts

1 Preheat the oven to 180°C. Grease a 22 cm fluted or 25 cm plain, deep-ring tin.
2 Beat together the eggs and sugar very well until light and fluffy. Continue beating while adding the oil slowly. Add the apple sauce.
3 Place the flour, cinnamon, mixed spice, cloves, nutmeg, salt and bicarb into a bowl, and stir to combine evenly. Gently but thoroughly fold into the egg mixture. Pour the batter into the prepared tin.
4 Bake for 45-50 minutes, until the cake is firm and a cake-tester comes out clean. Sprinkle with brandy, rum or sherry, and allow to cool for a few minutes. Turn out onto a wire rack.
5 For the topping, soften the caramel in a bowl in the microwave on Medium for 30-60 seconds. Alternatively, soften in a small saucepan over medium heat. Spread evenly onto the cake and sprinkle with chopped nuts.

GOURMET FRUIT LOAF

Serves 20

This loaf has a dense, fruity, nutty texture. Serve fresh from the oven, or keep refrigerated in an airtight container for up to a month.

100 g (250 ml) hazelnuts
150 g dried apricots
150 g dried smyrna figs
200 g (350 ml) bleached sultanas
200 g (250 ml) sugar
5 eggs
15 ml brandy
180 g (375 ml) Golden Cloud cake flour
  pinch salt
200 ml milk
icing sugar for dusting

1 Preheat the oven to 180°C. Line a medium (26 cm) loaf tin with nonstick baking paper or greased waxed paper.
2 Roast and skin the hazelnuts (see page 12). Leave them whole. Cut the apricots and figs into thin strips and cut up finely. Mix in the sultanas.
3 Beat together the sugar and eggs with an electric mixer, until very light and fluffy. Add the nuts and fruit, brandy, flour and salt, and beat in, adding the milk gradually to make an evenly blended, heavy batter.
4 Spoon the batter into the tin, smooth the top and bake for about 50 minutes, until the cake is golden brown and a cake-tester comes out clean. Turn out onto a wire rack and dust with icing sugar. Cool completely. Store in an airtight container.

COOK'S NOTES
• This fruit loaf lasts very well, but in very hot or humid weather refrigeration is recommended. Individually wrap sliced fingers for lunchboxes.
• Make two smaller loaves or mini loaves as gifts or for freezing. Adjust the baking time accordingly for smaller cakes.

COURGETTE LOAF

Serves 12–16

Courgettes (also called zucchini or baby marrows) make a tempting teabread with a pleasing texture and lightly spiced flavour.

2 eggs
125 ml sunflower oi
150 g (200 ml) sugar
5 ml vanilla essence
100 g (250 ml) grated courgettes
50 g (125 ml) pecan nuts, coarsely chopped
180 g (375 ml) Golden Cloud cake flour
1 ml salt
2 ml bicarbonate of soda
5 ml baking powder
5 ml ground cinnamon
icing sugar for dusting

1 Preheat the oven to 160°C. Generously grease a small (23 cm) loaf tin.
2 Place the eggs, oil, sugar and vanilla essence into a mixing bowl, and beat well by hand for 2 minutes. Stir in the courgettes and nuts, then add the flour, salt, bicarb, baking powder and cinnamon, and mix well until evenly blended.
3 Spoon the mixture into the prepared tin and bake for about 1 hour, until the cake is browned and a cake-tester comes out clean. Allow to cool in the tin for 5 minutes, then turn out onto a wire rack to cool completely.

COOK'S NOTE
For a delicious courgette and carrot loaf substitute grated carrot for half of the courgettes.

INDONESIAN SPICE & CHOCOLATE-CHIP CAKE

Serves 10–12

200 g (225 ml) butter or hard
  margarine, softened
200 g (250 ml) castor sugar
4 eggs
200 g (350 ml) Golden Cloud
  self-raising flour
120 g (250 ml) Golden Cloud cake flour
pinch salt
175 ml milk
5 ml ground cinnamon
5 ml mixed spice
5 ml vanilla essence
125–250 ml chocolate chips
icing sugar for dusting

1 Preheat the oven to 180°C. Generously grease a 22 cm fluted or 25 cm plain, deep-ring tin or a medium (26 cm) loaf tin.
2 Place the butter or margarine and castor sugar into a mixing bowl or the bowl of a food processor, and beat well or process for a few seconds, until creamed. Add the eggs, flours, salt, milk, cinnamon, mixed spice and vanilla essence, and beat well or process for 30 seconds to a smooth batter.
3 Add the chocolate chips and beat, or process, using the pulse action, until just combined. The chocolate chips should not become too finely chopped. Spoon the batter into the tin and smooth the top.
4 Bake for 45 minutes, until the cake is firm and golden brown and a cake-tester comes out clean. Allow the cake to cool in the tin for 5 minutes. Loosen, turn out carefully onto a wire rack, and allow to cool completely. Place onto a plate and dust with icing sugar.

COOK'S NOTES
• The cake lasts for several days in an airtight container.
• Add 125–250 ml pecan nuts to the chocolate chips, or instead of the chocolate chips.
• If you wish to pretty the cake up a bit, drizzle icing glaze decoratively over it when it has cooled. Sift 250 ml icing sugar into a bowl, add about 30 ml lemon juice, milk, coffee or brandy, and mix to a soft glaze.

CARIBBEAN CHOCOLATE RING CAKE

Serves 10–12

100 g (100 ml) butter or hard
   margarine, cut into cubes and
   softened
2 medium to large, very ripe bananas,
   peeled
2 eggs
50 ml buttermilk or sour cream
30 ml desiccated coconut, ground
   almonds or crumbed ginger biscuits
140 g (250 ml) Golden Cloud
   self-raising flour
140 g (175 ml) white or brown sugar
2 ml bicarbonate of soda
50 ml cocoa powder
pinch salt
5 ml vanilla essence

TOPPING

icing sugar for dusting, or half the
   recipe for Chocolate Glaze (any
   variation, see page 80)
lightly roasted nibbed almonds

1 Preheat the oven to 180°C. Grease a 22 cm fluted or 25 cm plain, deep-ring tin.
2 Place the butter or margarine, bananas, eggs, buttermilk or sour cream, coconut or almonds or biscuit crumbs, flour, sugar, bicarb, cocoa, salt and vanilla essence into the bowl of a food processor, and process for 1 minute, scraping the sides once if necessary. If using an electric mixer, first mash the bananas well before adding to the remaining ingredients in the bowl. Mix for 3 minutes.
3 Spoon the mixture into the tin, and smooth the top. Make the centre slightly hollow to compensate for rising while baking. Bake for about 30 minutes, until the cake is firm and a cake-tester comes out clean. Allow the cake to cool in the tin for a few minutes, then turn out onto a wire rack to cool completely.
4 Place the cake onto a plate, and dust lightly with icing sugar or coat evenly with glaze. Sprinkle with nuts if you wish.

COOK'S NOTES
• The flavour improves if this cake is kept sealed and refrigerated for a day or two.
• To make a larger, more luxurious chocolate cake, prepare a double quantity of batter and bake it in two 26 cm cake tins. Fill with whipped cream or Chocolate Butter Cream (page 82), and cover with a glaze of your choice. Decorate with Chocolate Curls or Leaves (page 11) or nut-filled chocolates.

CLASSIC CAKES

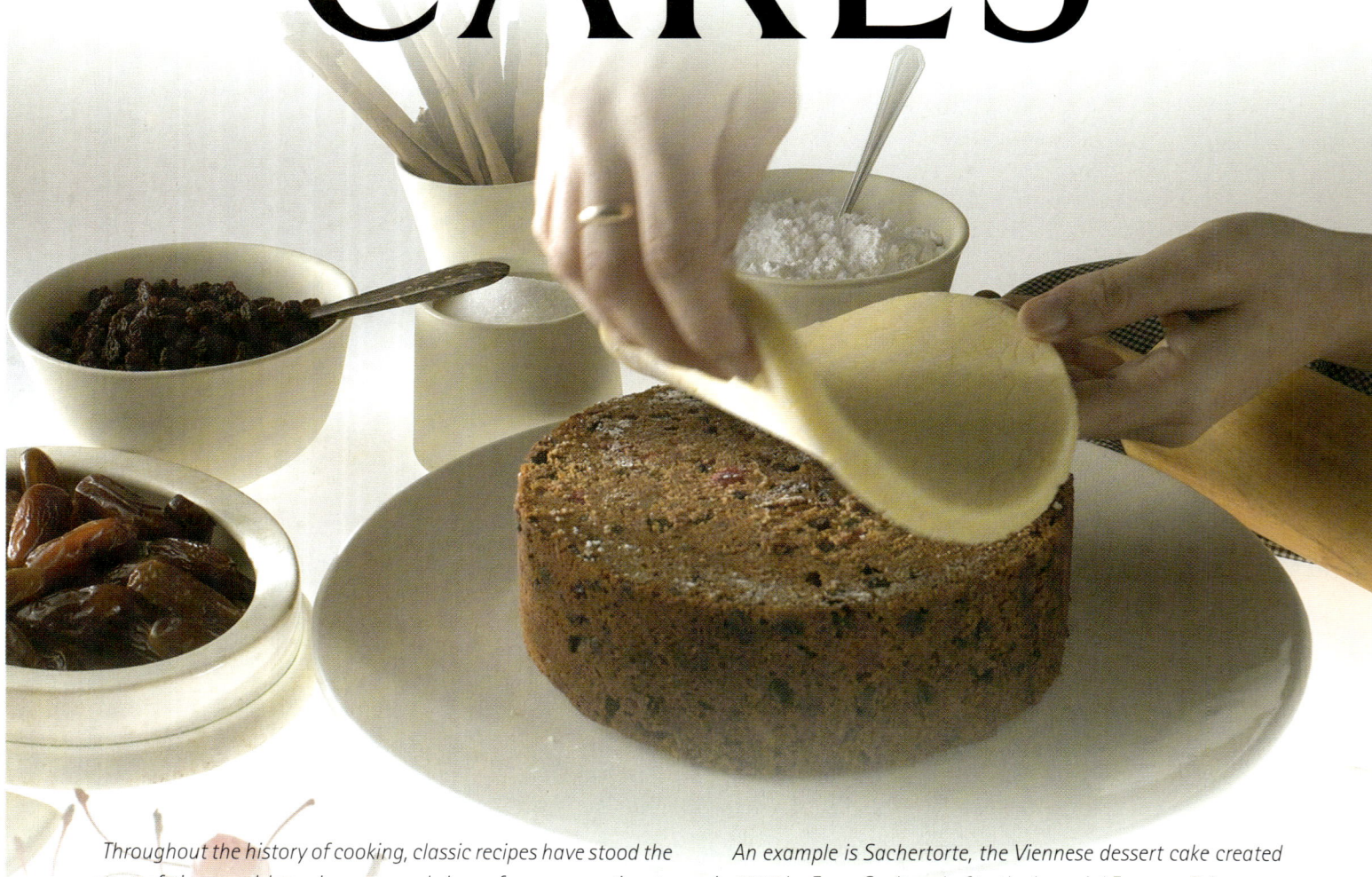

Throughout the history of cooking, classic recipes have stood the test of time, and have been passed down from generation to generation, and made over and over again. Baking is no exception, and books are filled with recipes for cakes that are so special that neither the changing seasons, the passing of time nor the vagaries of food fashion diminish their universal appeal.

Many have a fascinating history. Some have been adapted through the years by bakers who have made adjustments to the original recipe to improve texture or appearance, or who have changed the size or simplified the method while retaining the essence of the creation.

An example is Sachertorte, the Viennese dessert cake created in 1832 by Franz Sacher, chef to the Imperial Emperor Prince von Metternich. This luscious cake is still used in competitions as a benchmark of a baker's skill, and served in the most elegant continental-style coffee shops all over the world.

You'll find a host of recipes for famous cakes in this chapter – amongst them, Coconut Angel Food Cake, Swiss Roll, Madeira Cake, Rich Fruit Cake, and many more. Use them to produce splendid, classic cakes in your own kitchen. Most plain cakes keep well in an airtight container for up to three days. Filled cakes can be refrigerated for as long as the fillings remain fresh.

Coconut Angel Food Cake page 60

Mocha Roll page 64

Rich Fruitcake page 67

BASIC SPONGE CAKE

Serves 10–12

135 g (280 ml) Golden Cloud cake flour
200 g (250 ml) sugar
pinch salt
15 ml baking powder
125 ml sunflower oil
125 ml water
5 ml vanilla essence
4 eggs
icing sugar for dusting (optional)

1 Preheat the oven to 180°C. If using a 25 cm deep-ring tin, wash and dry well; don't grease it. For a layer cake, generously grease two 22 cm springform cake tins. For a loaf cake, grease one medium (26 cm) loaf tin.

2 Place the flour, sugar, salt, baking powder, oil, water and vanilla essence into the mixing bowl of an electric mixer, and beat at low speed for about 3 minutes.

3 Separate the eggs. Place the yolks into the batter and beat until just blended. In a separate, large mixing bowl, beat the whites until firm and glossy. Add to the batter, and mix in gently but thoroughly.

4 Pour the batter into the tin/s and knock gently on a hard surface to release air bubbles. Bake for 20–25 minutes (layer cake), or 30–35 minutes (ring cake or loaf), until the cake is golden and firm, and a cake-tester comes out clean. Remove the tin/s from the oven. Watchpoint: it's essential to bake this cake correctly. If undercooked the sponge will collapse; if overcooked the cake will be dry.

5 If you have used a deep-ring tin, turn over carefully and allow the cake to cool in the tin for at least 20 minutes to ensure perfect texture. Or loosen the sides of the cakes in the springform tins, and allow to cool for a few minutes before releasing the spring. Turn onto wire racks, remove the bases and allow to cool. Or, carefully loosen the sides of the loaf, knock the tin and shake the loaf out onto a wire rack. Dust with icing sugar.

SPONGE CAKE VARIATIONS

Chocolate Sponge Cake
Replace 30 ml of the flour with 50 ml cocoa powder. Fill and decorate with Sweetened Whipped Cream (page 80) and Chocolate Shavings, or Chocolate Curls (page 11). Suitable icings include Chocolate Butter Icing (page 81), Butter Cream (page 82), or Chocolate Milk-based Butter Cream (page 82).

Caramel Sponge Cake
Caramelise 50 ml of the sugar in a small saucepan over low heat. Add the water to dissolve the caramel. Make up to 125 ml with water. Beat with the other ingredients as described in step 2. Fill and decorate the cake with whipped Caramel Cream (page 81) scattered with toasted flaked almonds (see page 12).

Cream Sponge Cake with Fruit
Fill and decorate the cake with whipped cream or Sweetened Whipped Cream (page 80) and fresh or tinned fruit.

Chocolate Flake Sponge Cake
Fold in 100 g Chocolate Shavings (page 11). Serve plain or ice and decorate with Sweetened Whipped Cream (page 80), Butter Cream (page 82) or Butter Icing (page 81).

Chocolate-chip Sponge Cake
To prevent chocolate chips from sinking, stabilise the batter by increasing the flour to 300 ml and beating the egg whites until very firm. Add 125 ml chocolate chips when folding together the egg white and batter. Serve the cake plain, or fill and decorate as preferred.

Marbled Sponge Cake
Pour half of the batter into the prepared tin. Mix 30 ml cocoa powder with a little boiling water, and mix into the remaining batter. Pour into the tin in a zigzag manner, then gently draw a knife through the batter to create a marbled effect.

Orange Sponge Cake
Replace half the water with freshly squeezed, strained orange juice and 5 ml finely grated orange zest. Ice with Butter Icing (page 81), or Butter Cream (page 82), replacing the vanilla essence with 15 ml orange juice and 5 ml finely grated orange zest.

Spicy Sponge Cake
Sift 10 ml ground cinnamon, 2 ml ground cloves, 2 ml grated nutmeg and 2 ml ground allspice with the flour. Serve plain, or with Sweetened Whipped Cream (page 80), or whipped Caramel Cream (page 81).

MADEIRA CAKE

Serves at least 12

This popular cake originated on the Portuguese island of Madeira, has a fine texture and wonderful flavour. It's a dream to mix and bake, even for inexperienced bakers, and wraps easily for cake sales or car journeys.

125 g (150 ml) butter or hard
    margarine, softened
200 g (400 ml) Golden Cloud cake flour
150 g (200 ml) sugar
10 ml baking powder
2 eggs
125 ml milk
7 ml vanilla essence
1 ml salt
icing sugar for dusting

1 Preheat the oven to 170°C. Grease a medium (26 cm) loaf tin.
2 Place all the ingredients for the cake into the bowl of an electric mixer, or into a mixing bowl, and beat until very smooth and creamy. It will take approximately 5 minutes with an electric mixer. Scrape the sides of the bowl twice during mixing.
3 Spoon the batter into the prepared tin and smooth the top, making it slightly hollow in the centre to compensate for rising.
4 Bake for about 40 minutes until the cake is light golden and firm, and a cake-tester comes out clean.
5 Knock the base of the tin and shake it gently from side to side to loosen the cake. Turn out onto a wire rack and allow to cool for about 10 minutes before dusting with icing sugar. Cool completely.

COOK'S NOTE

Store at room temperature for up to 3 days, or refrigerate if the weather is hot and humid. The cake freezes very well if wrapped in foil. Thaw and reheat in the foil for 15 minutes at 180°C. Open the foil, switch off the oven and leave the cake in the oven for 5 minutes more.

MADEIRA CAKE VARIATIONS

Madeira Almond Cake
Add 2 ml almond essence to the batter, and sprinkle about 50 g flaked, or ribbed almonds on top.

Madeira Cherry Cake
Stir 80 g halved glacé cherries into the batter.

Madeira Coconut Cake
Stir 50 g (125 ml) desiccated coconut and a few drops of almond essence into the batter.

Madeira Fruitcake
Add about 50 g (125 ml) sultanas, raisins, currants or mixed fruit to the batter towards the end of the beating process. Chopped nuts can be added as well.

Madeira Ginger Cake
Replace the white sugar with brown sugar, and add ½ ml bicarbonate of soda, 10 ml ground ginger, 2 ml ground cinnamon and 2 ml mixed spice to the dry ingredients.

Madeira Lemon Cake
Replace the vanilla essence with 15 ml lemon juice and 10 ml finely grated zest.

Madeira Sherry Cake
Replace the white sugar with caramel sugar, replace 60 ml of the milk with sherry, and add a pinch of grated nutmeg.

Madeira Granadilla Cake
Use 30 ml of the syrup of a 185 g tin of granadilla pulp in the cake, and reduce the milk to 100 ml. Add the remainder of the tin to Granadilla Butter Icing (page 81).

Madeira Spice Cake
Replace the white sugar with brown sugar and add to the dry ingredients ½ ml bicarbonate of soda, 5 ml mixed spice, 5 ml ground cinnamon, 2 ml ground ginger and 1 ml grated nutmeg.

Madeira Cupcakes
Line 24 cups of two muffin tins with paper cups and divide the basic batter (or any of the variations) between them. Bake for about 20 minutes, until the cakes are golden and firm but not dry. Serve plain, dust with icing sugar or finish with Butter Icing (page 81).

COCONUT ANGEL FOOD CAKE

Serves 10–12

75 g (150 ml) Golden Cloud cake flour
35 g (75 ml) cornflour
80 g (100 ml) sugar
30 g (100 ml) desiccated coconut
300 ml egg whites (approximately 10)
2 ml salt
5 ml cream of tartar
120 g (150 ml) sugar
30 ml water
7 ml vanilla essence
2 ml almond essence
FILLING AND TOPPING
250 ml Butter Cream (page 82)
30 ml icing sugar
2 ml ground cinnamon

1 Preheat the oven to 170°C.
2 Sift together the flour and cornflour twice to aerate. Add the first measure of sugar, and the coconut, and stir lightly to combine.
3 Place the egg whites, salt and cream of tartar into the bowl of an electric mixer, and beat well with the balloon whisk, until firm. Gradually add the second measure of sugar, beating until stiff and glossy.
4 Add the water, vanilla and almond essences, and beat for a few seconds. Sprinkle the flour mixture onto the meringue, and beat or fold in very gently, until evenly distributed. Don't overbeat, or the meringue may collapse.
5 Turn the mixture into an ungreased 25 cm deep-ring tin, smooth the top and bake for 35–40 minutes, until the cake is golden brown and firm, and a cake-tester comes out clean. Switch off the oven, open the door and allow the cake to cool in the oven for 10 minutes. Remove from the oven and allow to cool in the tin for at least 10 minutes more. Remove the cake carefully from the tin, and place onto a wire rack to cool completely
6 Cut the cake into 2/3 layers: fill with Butter Cream. Dust with icing sugar and cinnamon.

SACHERTORTE

Serves 12–16

One of life's greatest pleasures is enjoying a slice of sachertorte with a cup of hot chocolate at the Sacher Hotel in Vienna. Making the cake at home is far cheaper!

200 g dark chocolate
7 eggs
120 g (150 ml) sugar
125 g (150 ml) butter or hard margarine, softened
100 g (200 ml) Golden Cloud cake flour
5 ml baking powder
pinch salt
APRICOT FILLING AND GLAZE
130 g (100 ml) smooth apricot jam
15 ml lemon juice or brandy
Chocolate Glaze (page 80)
GARNISH
50 g dark chocolate

1 Preheat the oven to 180°C. Line the base of a 24 cm springform tin with baking paper. Grease the paper and the sides of the tin.
2 Melt the chocolate (see page 11). Stir, and set aside.
3 Separate the eggs. Place the yolks into a small bowl, and the whites into a separate, large mixing bowl. Beat the egg whites until stiff.
4 Place the sugar and butter or margarine into a mixing bowl, or the bowl of an electric mixer, and beat very well until extremely creamy and light.
5 Add the egg yolks one at a time, beating well after each addition. Pour in the melted chocolate, beating constantly. Sift in the flour, baking powder and salt, and beat very slowly and gently, until just combined.
6 Add a quarter of the egg white to the batter and fold in to lighten it. Add the remaining egg white, and fold in lightly until evenly combined. Pour into the prepared tin and smooth the top, making t slightly hollow in the centre to compensate for rising.
7 Place the tin into the oven, and reduce the temperature to 170°C. Bake for about 45 minutes, until the cake is firm and a cake-tester comes out clean. Allow to cool in the tin for 5 minutes. Turn out onto a wire rack and cool completely. Cut horizontally into two even layers, and trim neatly if the cake has risen in the centre.
8 Prepare the apricot glaze: heat the jam and lemon juice or brandy gently in a small saucepan until just melted.
9 Turn the base of the cake upside down to use for the top layer; it has the smoothest surface. Brush glaze over both layers, covering tops and sides. Sandwich together.
10 Pour the cool chocolate glaze onto the cake, using a small, warm spatula to smooth the top and sides, sealing the cake completely. Cool until set.
11 Melt the garnish chocolate (see page 11). Fill an icing bag fitted with a plain, 5 mm nozzle. Write the name 'Sacher' on the cake in your very best handwriting! Allow to set.

COOK'S NOTES
• Use the best quality chocolate you can afford – the better the chocolate the better the cake!
• Bake the cake at least a day in advance; the flavour and texture improve if it has time to mellow. Store in a large, airtight container, opened a little if refrigerated to prevent moisture from forming on the glaze.

BLACK FOREST CAKE

Serves 10–12

125 g (150 ml) butter or hard margarine
6 eggs
200 g (250 ml) castor sugar
5 ml vanilla essence
60 g (125 ml) Golden Cloud cake flour
40 g (125 ml) cocoa powder

CHERRY CREAM FILLING AND TOPPING
60 ml kirsch
600 g stoned, drained cherries
  (approximate quantity;
   see Cook's notes)
500 ml cream
25 g (50 ml) icing sugar
1 ml vanilla essence

GARNISH
Chocolate Curls and Shavings (page 11)
reserved cherries

1 Preheat the oven to 180°C. Line the bases of two 22 cm springform tins with baking paper or waxed paper. Grease the paper and the side of the tins. Melt the butter or margarine (see page 11).

COOK'S NOTES
• The classic version of this cake is made with bottled German sour cherries that don't stain the cream. Morello cherries and tinned, stoned red cherries are good substitutes. If stoned black cherries are used the cake should be completed just before serving. Cherries are available in different sized jars or tins, which is why only an approximate quantity has been suggested.
• Mix the cherry syrup with cornflour (15 ml cornflour per 125 ml syrup) in a small saucepan, and boil, stirring until thick. Allow to cool and serve with the cake.

2 Place the eggs, castor sugar and vanilla essence into the bowl of an electric mixer, and beat until very pale and thick. Sift in the flour and cocoa, and fold in gently. Add the melted butter or margarine and fold in.
3 Pour the batter into the prepared tins, and bake for about 18 minutes, until the cake has risen and set in the centre, and a cake-tester comes out clean. Allow to cool in the tins for 5 minutes then remove carefully and place onto wire racks to cool completely.
4 Cut the layers horizontally, and sprinkle each layer with the kirsch. Beat the cream, icing sugar and vanilla essence until stiff. Drain and dry the cherries. Reserve 8–10 cherries.
5 To assemble the cake, fill with whipped cream and cherries. Cover the top with cream and decorate with Chocolate Curls and Shavings, and reserved cherries.

CHIFFON CAKE

Serves 10–12

A classic cake that is simple to prepare as long as the method is carried out correctly.

3 eggs
1 extra egg white (optional)
1 ml cream of tartar
120 g (150 ml) castor sugar
150 g (300 ml) Golden Cloud cake flour
60 g (80 ml) castor sugar
10 ml baking powder
1 ml salt
75 ml sunflower oil
125 ml water
5 ml vanilla essence
10 ml finely grated lemon zest (optional)
FILLING AND TOPPING (optional)
250 ml cream
10 ml castor sugar
fresh fruit (berries, mango, kiwi fruit, or
    drained, tinned fruit such as
    pineapple chunks or stoned cherries)
CHOCOLATE TOPPING
100 g dark chocolate
50 ml cream
1 ml vanilla essence

1 Preheat the oven to 180°C. Wash and dry a
   25 cm deep-ring tin. Do not grease the tin.
2 Separate the eggs. Place the yolks into a
   small jug and set aside. Place the whites and
   the extra white (if using) into a large mixing
   bowl, and beat with the cream of tartar until
   stiff. Gradually beat in the first measure of
   castor sugar, until stiff and glossy.
3 Sift the flour, the second measure of castor
   sugar, the baking powder and salt into a
   mixing bowl, or the bowl of an electric mixer.
   Make a hollow and add the egg yolks, oil,
   water, vanilla essence and lemon zest. Beat
   until just smooth. Don't overmix.
4 Pour the yolk mixture onto the egg white
   and gently fold in. Pour into the prepared tin.
5 Place the tin into the oven, reduce the
   temperature to 160°C, and bake for about

50 minutes, until the cake is golden and firm
and a cake-tester comes out clean. Don't
open the oven before the cake is done; it's
very delicate and may collapse.
6 Turn the tin over carefully and place gently
   onto a worktop; the rim will support it and
   allow air circulation. Cooling the cake upside
   down in the tin prevents shrinkage. When
   completely cold, loosen the sides with a
   spatula and lift out the cake. Loosen from the
   base and funnel. Turn out onto a wire rack.
7 Whip the filling cream stiffly and beat in the
   castor sugar. Cut the cake in layers
   horizontally, and fill with cream and fruit.
8 Roughly chop the topping dark chocolate
   into a bowl with the cream and vanilla
   essence. Microwave on Medium-low for
   about 3 minutes, until soft. Beat well. Pour
   and spread onto the cake.

COOK'S NOTE

If you don't possess a deep-ring tin , bake the batter in two generously greased 22 cm springform tins for about 35 minutes. Cool completely in the tins before removing.

CHIFFON CAKE VARIATIONS

Chocolate-chip Chiffon Cake
Add 30 g (50 ml) mini chocolate chips
or chopped dark or milk chocolate to the
bowl before folding together the egg white
and egg yolk mixtures.
Chocolate Chiffon Cake
Omit the lemon zest and replace 50 ml of the
flour with 75 ml sifted cocoa powder.
Mocha Chiffon Cake
Omit the lemon zest and replace 50 ml of the
flour with 75 ml sifted cocoa powder. Add
10 ml instant coffee granules as well, or
substitute cold, prepared coffee for the water.
Orange Chiffon Cake
Omit the vanilla essence and lemon zest.
Replace the water with the juice of 1 orange
made up to 125 ml with cold water. Add
10 ml finely grated orange zest as well.
Spicy Chiffon Cake
Add 2 ml ground cinnamon, 2 ml ground
ginger, 1 ml grated nutmeg and 1 ml mixed
spice to dry ingredients before sifting.
Pineapple Chiffon Cake
Replace the water with unsweetened
pineapple juice. Fill and top the cake with
whipped cream and garnish with pineapple
chunks. Or use Egg Yolk Butter Icing
(page 83), flavoured with
a few drops of pineapple essence.

SWISS ROLL

Serves 12–16

Perfection depends on following instructions meticulously!

4 eggs
120 g (150 ml) castor sugar
50 ml cold water
5 ml vanilla essence
120 g (250 ml) Golden Cloud cake flour
10 ml baking powder
pinch salt
granulated sugar or castor sugar
    for sprinkling
250 g (200 ml) apricot jam

1 Preheat the oven to 180°C. Line a medium baking tray with ungreased baking paper or well-greased waxed paper, allowing the paper to extend over the edges.
2 Separate the eggs. Beat the whites until stiff and set aside. Beat together the yolks and castor sugar in an electric mixer for 6–8 minutes until thick and pale yellow. Gently beat in the water and vanilla essence.
3 Sift together the flour, baking powder and salt. Sift again onto the egg mixture. Beat until just combined. Add the egg white, and fold in gently until evenly blended.
4 Spoon the batter into the baking tray evenly, filling right to the corners. Bake for 12–15 minutes, until the sponge is pale golden and just firm to the touch.
5 Meanwhile, sprinkle a clean tea towel with water, and roll to dampen all over. Place onto a worktop, and sprinkle with sugar.
6 Turn the cake out onto the cloth, remove the tray and cover the cake (don't remove the paper) with another cloth. Leave for about 5 minutes for the steam to soften the edges of the cake.
7 Carefully peel off the paper. Spread the jam onto the warm cake, and roll up gently with the aid of the cloth. Allow to cool while wrapped in the cloth. Sprinkle with extra sugar just before serving.

SWISS ROLL VARIATIONS

Spiced Swiss Roll
Add 5 ml ground cinnamon and 1 ml mixed spice or ground cloves to the flour.
Granadilla Swiss Roll
Substitute 50 ml granadilla pulp for the water and fill and ice the cake with Granadilla Butter Icing (page 81).
Chocolate Swiss Roll
Replace 30 ml of the cake flour with 30 ml sifted cocoa powder. Fill the cooled roll with Chocolate Whipped Cream (page 80), or Butter Cream (page 82). Dust with icing sugar or ice with Chocolate Glaze (page 80).
Cherry-filled Swiss Roll
Drain and stone a 410 g tin of red cherries. Place into a small saucepan with 30 ml cornflour and 15 ml medium-dry sherry. Bring to the boil, stirring until clear and thickened. Allow to cool. Spread the cherry mixture onto the cake, smooth Sweetened Whipped Cream (page 80), onto the cherries, and roll up the cake.

COOK'S NOTES
• Swiss Roll is best if filled within an hour of baking, while it's pliable enough to unroll, fill and roll up again.
• Leftover Swiss Roll is delicious in trifle.

MOCHA ROLL

Serves 12–16

A cake to serve at any celebration.
Prepare and chill the butter cream for a while
before completing the cake.

Swiss Roll (page 63,
    exclude the jam filling)
MOCHA BUTTER CREAM
80 g (100 ml) castor sugar
125 ml water
3 egg yolks
30 ml instant coffee granules
2 ml cocoa powder
5 ml brandy
2 ml vanilla essence
200 g (225 ml) butter or hard
    margarine, cut into cubes
    and softened
CHOCOLATE ALMOND GARNISH
50 g dark chocolate, melted
    (see page 11),
    Chocolate Leaves
    or Chocolate Curls (page 11)
roasted slivered or nibbed almonds
    (see page 12)
red glacé cherries (optional)
chocolate coffee beans (optional)

1 Make the Swiss Roll and roll up to cool.
2 To make the Mocha Butter Cream, place
   the castor sugar and water into a small
   saucepan, and cook over moderate heat,
   stirring until melted. Boil gently for about
   5 minutes until the syrup thickens
   and darkens and reduces by one-third.
3 Place the egg yolks into the bowl of an
   electric mixer. Beat very well until foamy
   and pale. Beat in the coffee, cocoa, brandy
   and vanilla essence. Pour in the hot syrup
   in a thin stream, beating constantly, until
   the mixture resembles a thick mousse. Allow
   to cool to room temperature.
4 Add in the butter or margarine bit by bit,
   beating well after each addition, until
   a smooth, light emulsion is obtained.

Refrigerate the butter cream for at least
30 minutes. Spoon about 50 ml into a piping
bag fitted with a rosette nozzle.
5 Unroll the cake and spread evenly with half
   the butter cream. Roll up and place onto
   a tray or board that will fit into the fridge.
   Ice the cake with the remaining butter
   cream, and pipe rosettes on top.

6 Refrigerate the cake for 1 hour for the
   butter cream to set. Carefully cover with
   foil, and refrigerate for at least another 2
   hours. Shortly before serving, melt the
   chocolate garnish (see page 11). Drizzle the
   melted chocolate over, and/or garnish with
   chocolate leaves or curls, almonds, cherries
   and chocolate coffee beans.

ALMOND PRALINE BUTTER CREAM ROLL

Serves 12–16

This extraordinary cake originated in Germany, where it was known as the Frankfurter Kranz, and was served at birthdays and other celebrations.

Swiss Roll (page 63, exclude the jam filling)
Almond Milk-based Butter Cream (page 82)

PRALINE

10 ml butter or hard margarine
80 g (100 ml) sugar
100 g (250 ml) slivered almonds

1 Make the Swiss Roll, following the steps as laid out on page 63, and roll up to cool. Make the Butter Cream.
2 To make the praline, grease a sheet of foil and place it onto a worktop. Place the butter or margarine and sugar into a flat, wide pan – nonstick if possible. Allow to melt over moderate heat, tilting the pan from side to side until the caramel starts to change colour. Add the almonds and cook, stirring constantly, until golden brown. Take care the caramel doesn't burn. Spread evenly onto the foil and allow to cool. Break the praline into small pieces, or crush lightly with a rolling pin.
3 Unroll the cake carefully and spread evenly with about half the Butter Cream. Roll up and place onto a tray or board that will fit into the fridge. Spread the cake evenly with the remaining Butter Cream, using a small spatula. Gently press the praline into the butter cream.
4 Refrigerate, uncovered, for at least 1 hour, to allow the butter cream to set.

COOK'S NOTE
Prepare the Butter Cream and praline in advance and make the cake at least a day beforehand, so that the cake, butter cream and praline blend nicely together.

GOLDEN CARROT CAKE

Serves 12–16

This well-loved classic cake is moist and light, and its natural golden colour results from a lack of bicarbonate of soda.

200 g (250 ml) sugar
3 eggs
250 ml sunflower oil
500 ml grated carrots
170 g (350 ml) Golden Cloud cake flour
7 ml baking powder
1 ml salt
100 g (250 ml) pecan nuts, chopped
   (or, for a more economical cake,
   use toasted muesli)
10–15 ml grated fresh ginger
5 ml ground cinnamon
icing sugar for dusting

1 Preheat the oven to 160°C. Grease a 22 cm springform tin, or a medium rectangular ovenproof dish.
2 Place the sugar, eggs and oil into the bowl of an electric mixer, and beat until well blended. Add all the remaining ingredients, and beat well until combined.
3 Spoon the batter evenly into the prepared tin or dish. Bake for 45 minutes, until the cake is firm to the touch and lightly browned, and a cake-tester comes out clean.
4 Remove the cake from the tin, and place onto a wire rack to cool completely. Dust lightly with icing sugar. Or, cool in the baking dish, dust with icing sugar and serve directly from the dish. Alternatively, serve with one of the suggested toppings or fillings. Keep the unfilled cake in the fridge for 5 days.

GOLDEN CARROT CAKE VARIATIONS

Mini Carrot Cakes
Fill generously greased ovenproof moulds, ramekins or jumbo muffin cups with the batter until two-thirds full. Place onto a baking tray and bake for about 30 minutes, until golden and firm to the touch. Allow to cool for 5 minutes, then loosen the cakes and turn out carefully.

OPTIONAL TOPPINGS AND FILLINGS

Caramel Cream Cheese (page 81)
Serve in a separate bowl or spoon over slices.
Caramel Cream (page 81)
Cut the cake in half horizontally, and use as a filling, or spoon over the completed cake.
Lemon Butter Icing (page 81)
More traditional and sweeter, and suitable to fill, ice and decorate the cake.

RICH FRUITCAKE

Serves at least 24

A moist dark fruitcake made with an interesting mix of dried fruit and other wonderful flavourings, and so attractive that the sides are left uncovered, with home-made almond paste (marzipan) on top.

125 g (200 g) finely chopped, stoned dates
125 g (200 ml) seedless raisins
125 g (200 ml) bleached sultanas
125 g red glacé cherries, halved
150 ml hot, strong black coffee
50 ml Kahlúa, brandy, rum or additional coffee
125 g (150 ml) butter or hard margarine
100 g (125 ml) sugar
2 eggs
150 g (125 ml) molasses
150 g (125 ml) strawberry jam
240 g (500 ml) Golden Cloud cake flour
2 ml salt
2 ml bicarbonate of soda
2 ml ground cinnamon
1 ml grated nutmeg
½ ml ground ginger
½ ml ground cloves
100 g pecan nuts or walnuts, very coarsely chopped

ALMOND PASTE
100 g (250 ml) ground almonds
65 g (125 ml) icing sugar
100 g (125 ml) castor sugar
15 ml brandy
10 ml lemon juice
1 ml almond essence
2 egg yolks
icing sugar for kneading and rolling

1 Place the fruit (as listed, or a combination thereof, made up to 500 g) into a mixing bowl. Pour over the coffee and liquor (if using), or both measures of coffee. Set aside for at least 1 hour for the fruit to absorb the flavours.

2 Preheat the oven to 150°C. Line the base of either a large loaf tin, deep fruitcake tin, 20 cm deep ovenproof dish, or 22 cm springform tin, with waxed paper or baking paper. The volume capacity of the tin/dish should be 2 litres. Generously grease the paper and sides of the tin or dish.

3 Place the butter or margarine and sugar into a bowl, or the bowl of an electric mixer, and beat very well until light and fluffy. Beat in the eggs, molasses and strawberry jam. Add the flour, salt, bicarb, and spices, and the fruit and nuts together with the liquid, and beat until evenly combined.

4 Turn the batter into the prepared tin or dish. Cover with heavy foil, greased well over the part that will come into contact with the batter. Bake for 2½ hours, until the cake is firm and a cake-tester comes out clean.

5 Allow the cake to cool (still covered), in the tin or dish for 5 minutes. Turn out onto the foil, and wrap in the foil while cooling to keep it moist. Leave the cake for several hours (up to a day is even better).

6 Place all the ingredients for the almond paste into a small bowl and mix well to a smooth paste. Turn out onto a surface sprinkled with icing sugar, and knead until smooth. Dust a rolling pin with icing sugar and roll out the paste evenly to fit the top of the cake. Cover the cake, trim the edges neatly and wrap in foil. When ready to serve, tie a festive ribbon around and garnish with ornaments and fresh holly leaves.

COOK'S NOTES
• Wrap the cake/s in foil, and keep for several weeks. If you plan to keep it for more than a week, sprinkle lightly with liqueur, rum or brandy. Make the almond paste when required, and decorate the cake/s no longer than a day before serving.
• If you don't wish to make your own almond paste use a tub of marzipan.
• Vary the fruit according to taste, making it up to 500 g. Fruitcake mix, chopped glacé fruit, dried figs, apricots, pears or peaches are all delicious.

SPECIAL OCCASION CAKES

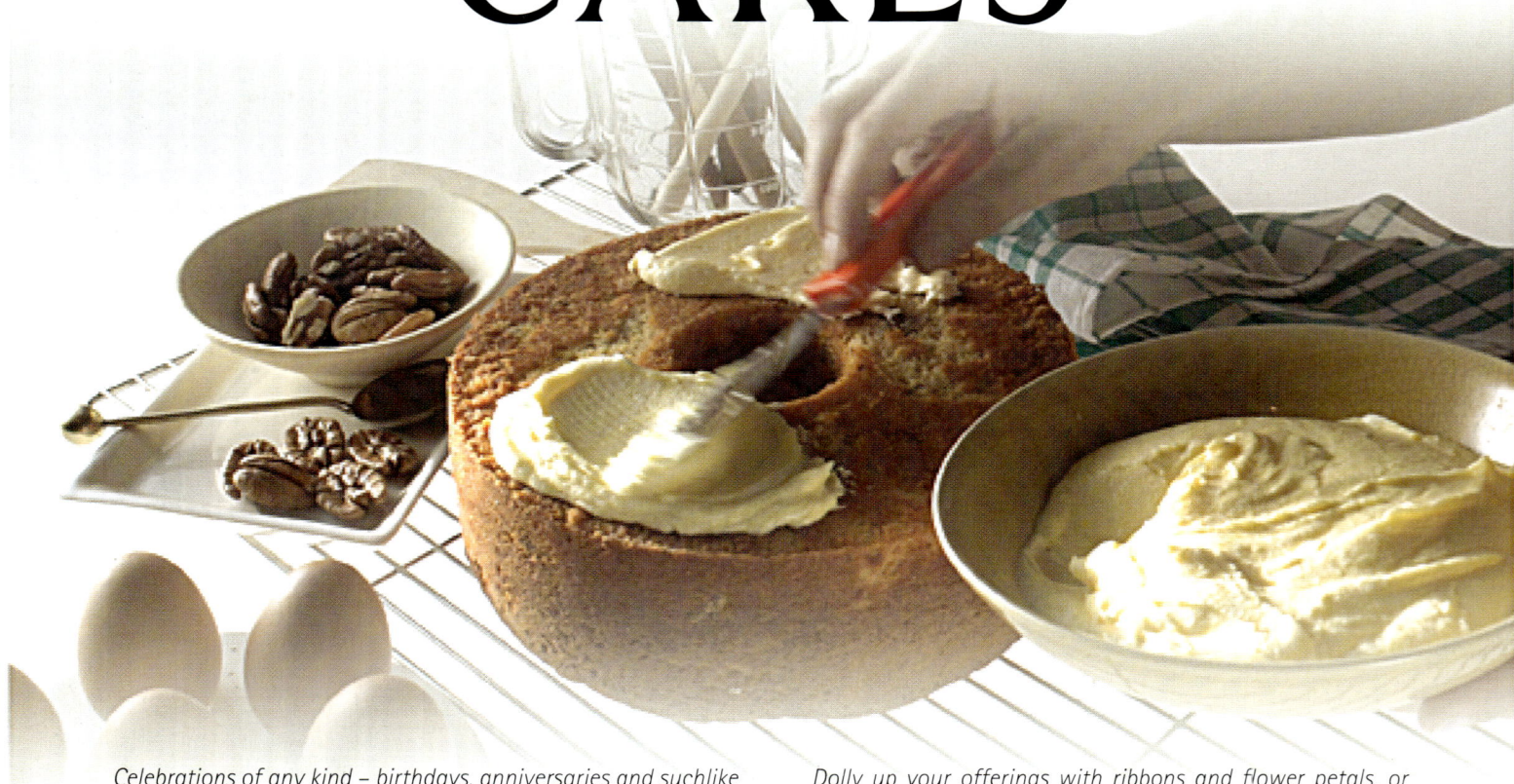

Celebrations of any kind – birthdays, anniversaries and suchlike – are associated with a special cake, baked with love and care.

Some of these cakes are complicated and fancy, and require a little extra time and effort to bake, while others are quite easy to mix but artistically decorated to fit the occasion. Some call for ingredients that are more extravagant, and methods that may, at first, seem slightly more complex than required for plainer cakes. Some are well-known, much-loved classics, while others are newer innovations. All are absolutely delicious.

Another thing that sets these recipes apart is the icings, frostings, fillings and garnishes that add an unusual and professional finishing touch to the product. This is where creative cooks can get carried away – and get away with it.

Dolly up your offerings with ribbons and flower petals, or decorate with candles and sparklers.

Many of the cakes in this section have their own icings and fillings, but all of them can be mixed and changed depending on personal preferences. At the end of this chapter you'll find a host of ideas for filling and decorating cakes; all of them – from sweetened, whipped cream to rich chocolate glazes and simple fruit finishes – can be used with any of the cakes in the book.

Serve any of these cakes as a delicious dessert to round off a meal. Spoon custard or fruit sauce onto the plate, pop a slice of cake on top, add a dollop of softly whipped cream or a scoop of ice cream, and finish off by dusting everything – the cake, the plate, the works – with sifted icing sugar or cocoa.

Mocha Mousse Roll page 73

Double White Cake page 72

Gooseberry Cake page 79

CHOC-NUT SPONGE CAKE

Serves 10–12

Nutty chocolate perks up a sponge to make an unbelievably moist and flavourful cake.

120 g (250 ml) Golden Cloud cake flour
200 g (250 ml) sugar
15 ml baking powder
pinch salt
125 ml sunflower oil
125 ml water
5 ml vanilla essence
4 eggs
200 g whole nut chocolate, grated

CHOCOLATE TOPPING
100 g dark, milk or white chocolate
10 ml butter or cream

1 Preheat the oven to 180°C. Use an ungreased, 25 cm loose-bottomed, deep-ring tin or grease a 22 cm fluted ring tin.
2 Place the flour, sugar, baking powder and salt into a mixing bowl. Add the oil, water and vanilla essence. Beat until just combined.
3 Separate the eggs. Add the yolks and grated chocolate to the flour mixture. Mix until combined. In a separate bowl, beat the whites until stiff, and fold into the flour mixture.
4 Pour the batter into the tin, and bake for about 40 minutes, until the cake is firm and a cake-tester comes out clean.
5 Remove the cake from the oven. If you've used a deep-ring tin, place upside down onto a wire rack to cool; if you've used a fluted ring pan, stand upright on the rack. Allow the cake to cool in the tin for 15 minutes.
6 Remove from the tin and place onto the rack to cool completely.
7 To make the topping: place the chocolate and butter or cream into a jug, and microwave on Medium for 2–3 minutes, until melted. Stir to blend evenly. Pour over the cake and allow to cool before serving.

COOK'S NOTE
Omit the chocolate topping and dust the cake with icing sugar.

TRIPLE-RICH SPONGE CAKE

Serves 12–16

A spectacular, rich sponge filled and topped with caramel, cream and chopped Crunchies.

7 eggs
250 g (325 ml) sugar
85 g (175 ml) Golden Cloud cake flour
85 g (175 ml) cornflour
pinch salt
50 g (50 ml) butter or hard margarine, melted
5 ml vanilla essence
few drops almond essence (optional)

CARAMEL FILLING
200 ml cream
5 ml gelatine
30 ml water
1/2 x 380 g tin caramel
50 g Crunchie chocolate bar

CARAMEL TOPPING
50 g Crunchie chocolate bar
200 g caramel chocolate
30 ml cream or milk

COOK'S NOTES
• After filling with cream, refrigerate the cake in an airtight container. Don't add the caramel chocolate coating and chopped Crunchie more than an hour before serving.
• To make a layer cake, bake it in two 22 cm loose-bottomed cake tins for about 35 minutes.
• To turn this into a simple cream cake, omit the filling and topping, and use Sweetened Whipped Cream (page 80). Garnish with berries, kiwi fruit or cubed fresh or tinned pineapple, if you wish.

1 Preheat the oven to 150°C. Grease a 25 cm deep-ring tin.
2 Separate the eggs, and place whites and yolks into separate bowls. Beat egg whites until firm but not dry. Gradually beat in one-third of the sugar, until stiff and glossy.
3 Add the remaining sugar to the egg yolks, and beat well until very pale and light. Sift together the flour, cornflour and salt. Add a tablespoonful at a time to the yolk mixture, beating continually to prevent lumps from forming.
4 Fold in the egg white. Stir in the melted butter or margarine until evenly blended. Stir in the vanilla essence, and almond essence (if using). Pour into the prepared tin and bake for about 50 minutes, until the cake is firm to the touch but hardly browned, and a cake-tester comes out clean.
5 Allow the cake to cool in the tin for at least 20 minutes to prevent shrinkage. Remove carefully and turn out onto a wire rack to cool completely. Cut in half horizontally.
6 To make the filling, whip the cream until stiff. Dissolve the gelatine in the water (see page 12). Stir in about 50 ml of the whipped cream. Gently stir the gelatine into the whipped cream, until evenly blended. Refrigerate for a few minutes, until just firm enough to hold shape.
7 Spread the caramel onto the bottom layer of the cake, then spread the cream onto the caramel. Refrigerate for about 10 minutes until set. Coarsely chop the Crunchie, sprinkle onto the cream, and cover with the top cake layer.
8 To make the topping, break the caramel chocolate into a jug and microwave on Medium for 2 minutes until it is soft. Add the cream or milk and stir until the mixture is smooth.
9 Spread the glaze onto the cake, allowing it to run down the sides. Coarsely chop the Crunchie and sprinkle onto the caramel while it is still soft. Allow the caramel to cool and set. If necessary, refrigerate the coated cake, uncovered, for a short while until ready to serve. Refrigerate any leftover cake in an airtight container.

1 Preheat the oven to 200°C. Generously
  grease two 22 cm springform cake tins.
2 Beat together the eggs and sugar for
  10 minutes with an electric mixer until very
  thick and pale.
3 Combine the oil, water, and vanilla and
  almond essences in a jug. Add half this liquid
  to the egg mixture, and beat in. Sift the
  flour, baking powder and salt on top, and
  beat in. Add the remaining liquid slowly,
  beating constantly, until just evenly blended.
4 Divide the batter between the prepared tins
  and bake for 15–20 minutes, until the cakes
  are golden and firm and a cake-tester comes
  out clean. Loosen the sides of the cake and
  allow to cool in the tins for 20 minutes. Turn
  out onto a wire rack and cool completely.
5 To make the white chocolate cream, melt
  the chocolate (see page 11). Mix about
  50 ml of the cream cheese with the egg yolk.
  Beat into the melted chocolate a teaspoonful
  at a time. Beat in the remaining cream
  cheese a tablespoonful at a time, beating
  well after each addition. Beat in the butter
  or margarine, a teaspoonful at a time,
  until smooth and thick. Beat in the vanilla
  essence. Refrigerate until firm enough
  to spread.
6 To complete the cake, sandwich the layers
  with approximately one-third of the filling.
  Ice the cake neatly with the remaining filling.
7 To garnish, make shavings with the white
  chocolate (see page 11). Press on top and
  around the cake, and refrigerate in a covered
  container until firm.
8 Place the cake onto a serving plate, and tie
  the ribbon around it. Add a sprig of greenery
  (use holly if it's Christmas time) if you like,
  or garnish with flowers and fresh fruit.

DOUBLE WHITE CAKE

Serves 12–16

*A tall and impressive white sponge cake filled
with delectable white-chocolate butter cream.*

4 eggs
300 g (375 ml) sugar
50 ml sunflower oil
250 ml water
5 ml vanilla essence
2 ml almond essence
250 g (500 ml) Golden Cloud cake flour
15 ml baking powder
pinch salt

WHITE CHOCOLATE CREAM
150 g white chocolate
500 g (500 ml) creamed cottage
  cheese
1 egg yolk
100 g (100 ml) butter or
  hard margarine (approximate
  amount), softened
5 ml vanilla essence
GARNISH
100 g white chocolate
1 metre decorative wide floral
  or parcel ribbon (optional)
green leaves, flowers, and fresh fruit
  (optional)

COOK'S NOTE
This cake tastes even better if it is made a
day or two in advance; the completed cake
can be refrigerated in an airtight container
for up to 5 days.

MOCHA MOUSSE ROLL

Serves 12–16

4 eggs
5 ml vanilla essence
150 g (200 ml) sugar
140 g (250 ml) Golden Cloud cake flour
5 ml baking powder
60 ml cocoa powder
pinch salt
100 ml water
castor sugar for sprinkling

MOCHA MOUSSE FILLING
50 g milk chocolate
50 g dark chocolate
50 ml milk
7 ml gelatine
50 ml water
2 eggs
15 ml brown sugar
2 ml instant coffee granules
2 ml vanilla essence
15–30 ml brandy
125 ml cream

CHOCOLATE TOPPING (OPTIONAL)
50 g dark chocolate
50 g butter or hard margarine, softened
5 ml vanilla essence
about 100 g (200 ml) icing sugar, sifted
Chocolate Leaves and Curls (page 11)

1 Preheat the oven to 180°C. Line a medium baking tray with nonstick baking paper, or greased waxed paper.
2 Beat together the eggs and vanilla essence in a food processor or with an electric mixer. Gradually beat in the sugar, until thick and pale. Sift the flour, baking powder, cocoa and salt on top, and beat in slowly while adding the water.
3 Pour the batter into the prepared tray and spread evenly. Bake for 12–15 minutes, until the cake is just firm to the touch; if baked too dry it will be hard to roll.
4 Lay out a dampened tea towel and sprinkle with castor sugar. Turn out the cake on top of the tea towel. Leave the paper on and cover the cake with another damp cloth for a few minutes to soften the cake. Carefully peel off the paper and roll up the cake with the aid of the towel. Allow to cool, wrapped in the cloth, for at least 30 minutes.
5 To make the filling, melt the chocolates with the milk (see page 11). Stir until smooth. Dissolve the gelatine in water (see page 12). Stir into the melted chocolate.
6 Separate the eggs. Beat the egg yolks, sugar and coffee with an electric beater, until quite thick and fluffy. Pour in the hot melted chocolate mixture and beat until smooth. Beat in the vanilla essence and brandy.
7 Beat the egg white in a large bowl until firm but not dry. In a separate bowl, beat the cream until stiff. Add the egg white and cream to the chocolate mixture, and fold together until evenly blended. Refrigerate for about 10 minutes, until slightly firm.
8 Unroll the cooled cake and spread the mousse on top. Roll up, trim the edges and refrigerate.
9 To make the topping, melt the chocolate. Stir in the butter or margarine, and sufficient icing sugar to form a spreadable glaze. Mix in the vanilla essence. Spread onto the cake, and draw decorative lines with a fork. Garnish with chocolate leaves and curls just before serving.

COOK'S NOTES
- To make a white chocolate mousse filling, replace the dark chocolate with white chocolate, replace the brown sugar with white, and omit the coffee granules.
- To make a white swiss roll for an all-white cake, replace the cocoa in the batter with 30 ml cake flour and prepare white chocolate mousse as explained above. Or make a white sponge roll and fill it with a dark chocolate mousse.
- Replace the brandy with Kahlúa; it's especially delicious if you plan to serve this cake as a dessert.

CARAMEL PECAN CREAM ROLL

Serves 10–12

CARAMEL CREAM
250 ml cream
50 g (60 ml) brown sugar
2 ml vanilla essence
4 glacé cherries (red or green), chopped
20 g (50 ml) coarsely chopped pecan nuts

PECAN NUT SPONGE
4 eggs
50 ml water
5 ml vanilla essence
200 g (250 ml) castor sugar
120 g (250 ml) Golden Cloud cake flour
5 ml baking powder
pinch salt
100 g evenly chopped pecan nuts
30 ml sugar
2 ml cinnamon

1 To make the caramel cream, place the cream and brown sugar into a small saucepan, and bring to the boil, stirring constantly. Reduce the heat and simmer very gently for 10 minutes. Pour into a bowl and stir in the vanilla essence. Cover and refrigerate until well chilled, preferably overnight.

2 Preheat the oven to 200°C. Line a medium baking tray with waxed paper, allowing the paper to extend over the sides of the tin. Grease well.

3 To make the sponge, separate the eggs; place the whites and yolks into separate bowls. Beat the water, vanilla essence and castor sugar into the yolks until thick and pale yellow. Beat the egg whites until stiff.

4 Combine the flour, baking powder, salt and nuts. Add to the yolk mixture, and fold in until evenly combined. Pour onto the beaten egg whites, and fold together gently.

5 Turn the batter into the prepared baking tray. Spread evenly, and bake for about 10 minutes, until the cake is lightly browned and firm to the touch.

6 Combine the sugar and cinnamon. Lay out a dampened tea towel and sprinkle with about two-thirds of the cinnamon sugar. Turn out the cake on top of the tea towel. Leave the paper on and cover the cake with another damp cloth for a few minutes to soften the cake. Carefully remove the paper and roll up the sponge with the aid of the cloth. Allow to cool, wrapped in the cloth for at least 30 minutes.

7 Beat the chilled caramel cream until stiff. Fold in the cherries and nuts. Unroll the cake, spread with the caramel cream, roll up and place onto a plate. Sprinkle with the remaining cinnamon sugar and refrigerate until required.

BRAZILIAN RING CAKE

Serves 12–16

250 g (280 ml) butter or hard
  margarine, softened
250 g (325 ml) sugar
120 g (150 ml) brown sugar
5 eggs
250 ml sour cream
125 ml brandy
300 g (600 ml) Golden Cloud cake flour
60 g (125 ml) Ace Super maize meal
10 ml baking powder
1 ml salt
5 ml ground cinnamon
2 ml grated nutmeg
200 g (375 ml) coarsely chopped
  brazil nuts

BRANDY GLAZE

30 ml butter or margarine, softened
130 g (250 ml) icing sugar
10 ml brandy
15 ml milk (approximate amount)

1 Preheat the oven to 160°C. Grease a 26 cm fluted ring tin or 25 cm deep-ring tin.
2 Beat together the butter or margarine and sugars in a food processor, or with an electric mixer, until light and fluffy. Add the eggs one by one, beating well after each addition. Beat in the sour cream and brandy.
3 Add the flour, maize meal, baking powder, salt, and spices, and beat until well blended. Add three-quarters of the nuts and fold in. Spoon the batter into the prepared tin, smooth the top and bake for about 1 hour, until the cake is firm to the touch and a cake-tester comes out clean. Allow to cool in the tin for 10 minutes. Loosen carefully and turn out onto a wire rack to cool completely.
4 To make the brandy glaze, mix the ingredients together, adding sufficient milk to make a thick, pourable consistency. Spread onto the cake. Garnish with remaining nuts.

> ## COOK'S NOTES
> • To make a fruit and pecan cake, use 75 g (125 ml) dried fruit. Increase the brandy to 200 ml and soak the fruit in it for 1 hour. Mix the fruit and brandy into the creamed butter or margarine and sugar mixture.
> • Use macadamias, pecans, almonds, hazels or mixed unsalted nuts, instead of brazil nuts.

PECAN PRALINE MOCHA CREAM CAKE

Serves 10–12

A classic sponge layer becomes a luxurious cake with a creamy filling and contrasting, nutty praline layers.
Outstanding as a dessert cake.

2 eggs
150 g (200 ml) sugar
30 ml sunflower oil
2 ml vanilla essence
125 ml water
120 g (250 ml) Golden Cloud cake flour
7 ml baking powder
pinch salt

PECAN PRALINE LAYERS
100 g (100 ml) butter or hard
　margarine, softened
80 g (100 ml) sugar
100 g coarsely chopped pecan nuts

MOCHA CREAM FILLING
250 ml cream
15 ml sugar
10 ml instant coffee granules
5 ml cocoa powder
5 ml vanilla essence or 15 ml coffee
　liqueur (Kahlúa)

CHOCOLATE TOPPING
50 g dark chocolate
75 ml milk

1 Preheat the oven to 200°C. Grease a 24 cm springform cake tin.
2 Beat together the eggs and sugar very well with an electric mixer until light and fluffy. Add the oil, vanilla essence and water, and beat in. Add the flour, baking powder and salt, and beat until just smooth.
3 Pour the batter into the prepared tin and bake for about 20 minutes, until the cake is firm and a cake-tester comes out clean. Loosen the sides and allow the cake to cool in the tin for 10 minutes. Remove carefully and cool completely on a wire rack. Cut in half horizontally.

4 To make the praline, line one large or two smaller baking trays with foil and draw two circles the size of the cake with the tip of a sharp-pointed knife; don't cut the foil.
5 Beat together the butter or margarine and sugar in a food processor or with an electric mixer, until creamy. Mix in the nuts. Spread the mixture onto the circles, leaving about 10 mm around the edge uncovered to allow for spreading while baking.
6 After baking the cake, place the praline into the oven. Reduce the temperature to 180°C and bake for about 18 minutes, until light golden brown. Take care: if baked too long, the praline will become too dark; if insufficiently baked it won't harden. If the praline spreads out wider than the circles, push it back into place with a knife. Allow to cool and harden before removing the foil.
7 For the mocha cream, place all the ingredients into a bowl and beat until quite stiff. Spread half onto the bottom layer of the cake. Cover with one praline layer, then the second layer of cake, the remaining cream and the second praline layer. Press down very gently.
8 To make the topping, melt the chocolate (see page 11). Mix in the milk. Drizzle thin streaks decoratively onto the praline. Place the completed cake into an airtight container and refrigerate for at least 2 hours before slicing. Keep refrigerated for up to 2 days.

COOK'S NOTES
- Substitute shelled, toasted hazelnuts or blanched almonds for pecans.
- For a plainer mocha cream cake, bake two sponge layers, omit the praline and fill and decorate with the cream and chocolate streaks.

COTTAGE CHEESE CAKE

Serves 10–12

Keep copies of this recipe handy when serving this cake; your guests will be sure to ask for it!

100 g (100 ml) butter or hard
    margarine, softened
250 g (325 ml) sugar
250 g (250 ml) cottage cheese
5 ml vanilla essence
4 eggs
240 g (500 ml) Golden Cloud cake flour
10 ml baking powder
1 ml salt
icing sugar for dusting
CHOCOLATE WALNUT TOPPING
50 g (125 ml) roughly chopped dark
    chocolate or chocolate chips
50 g (125 ml) roughly chopped
    walnuts or pecan nuts
5 ml ground cinnamon

1 Preheat the oven to 180°C. Line the base
  of a 24 cm springform tin with baking paper
  or waxed paper. Grease the paper as well as
  the sides of the tin.
2 Beat the butter or margarine and sugar very
  well in a food processor or with an electric
  mixer, until creamy. Beat in the cottage
  cheese and vanilla essence. Add the eggs
  one by one, beating well after each addition.
3 Add the flour, baking powder and salt, and
  beat until just evenly combined. Turn the
  batter into the prepared tin.
4 Mix together the topping ingredients and
  sprinkle onto the cake. Make a few squiggles
  with a fork to slightly mix the topping into
  the batter. As it bakes, the layers will blend
  together to create an interesting effect.
5 Bake for about 45 minutes, until the cake
  is set and lightly browned, and a cake-tester
  comes out clean. Remove from the oven and
  allow the cake to cool in the tin for about
  10 minutes. Remove from the tin and place
  onto a wire rack to cool completely. Dust
  with icing sugar.

COOK'S NOTE
For a white chocolate poppy seed cheese cake, replace the dark chocolate with white chocolate, the walnuts with 30 ml poppy seeds, and reduce the cinnamon to 1 ml.

COOK'S NOTES
• Marzipan needs to be fresh to blend well. For a larger cake, double the recipe and bake it in a 25 cm deep-ring tin. Increase the baking time to 45 minutes.
• For a richer cake glaze it with chocolate: melt together 100 g dark chocolate, 50 ml milk and 10 ml butter or margarine. Stir to blend and coat the cake evenly. Sprinkle roasted, flaked almonds on top. Store in an airtight container. (See pages 11–12 for tips on how to melt chocolate and roast nuts.)
• For a festive cake add to the batter 50 g of your favourite cake-fruit: sultanas, glacé cherries, fruitcake mix or chopped dried fruit. If you wish to add more fruit, soak it in brandy in advance, to prevent the cake from becoming dry.

MARZIPAN SPONGE CAKE

Serves 8–10

Exceptional and different, whether presented plain or glazed with chocolate and nuts, or baked with fruit and dusted with icing sugar, as described in the Cook's notes.

125 g marzipan, crumbled
125 g (150 ml) butter or hard
    margarine, cut into cubes
    and softened
100 g (125 ml) sugar
3 eggs
2 ml vanilla essence
few drops almond essence
120 g (250 ml) Golden Cloud cake flour
2 ml baking powder
$\frac{1}{2}$ ml salt
icing sugar for dusting

1 Preheat the oven to 180°C. Generously
  grease a medium (26 cm) loaf tin or 22 cm
  ovenproof glass ring mould.
2 Place the marzipan, butter or margarine
  and sugar into the bowl of a food processor
  or electric mixer, and process or beat until
  quite smooth.
3 Add the eggs one at a time and beat.
  Add the vanilla and almond essences.
  Continue processing or beating until very
  light and fluffy.
4 Add the flour, baking powder and salt,
  and process or beat just until combined.
  Spoon into the prepared tin or mould
  and smooth the top.
5 Place into the oven and reduce the
  temperature to 160°C. Bake for about
  35 minutes, until the cake is golden
  and a cake-tester comes out clean.
  Allow the cake to cool in the tin or mould
  for 5 minutes, then loosen carefully and
  turn out onto a wire rack to cool
  completely. Place onto a plate, and dust
  with icing sugar.

BEET AND CARROT CAKE

Serves 12

*This will knock the socks off any other carrot
cake you have tasted!*

3 eggs
300 g (375 ml) sugar
175 ml sunflower oil
5 ml vanilla essence
60 ml hot water
240 g (500 ml) Golden Cloud cake flour
15 ml baking powder
1 ml salt
5 ml ground cinnamon
½ ml grated nutmeg
200 g (500 ml) finely grated carrot
100 g (250 ml) finely grated beetroot
50 g (125 ml) coarsely chopped pecan
nuts or walnuts

1 Preheat the oven to 180°C. Generously
grease a 25 cm deep-ring tin.
2 Separate the eggs. Place the yolks into a
large mixing bowl or a food processor, and
add the sugar, oil, vanilla essence and hot
water. Beat or process until just combined.
3 Add the flour, baking powder, salt and spices;
beat or process until smooth. Add the carrot,
beetroot and nuts; mix until just combined.
4 Beat the egg whites until stiff. Fold into the
batter until evenly combined. Pour into the
prepared tin and bake for 45–50 minutes,
until the cake is golden brown and firm and
a cake-tester comes out clean.
5 Allow the cake to cool in the tin for at least
10 minutes. Remove carefully and place
onto a plate.

COOK'S NOTES

- Use grated courgettes instead of beetroot.
- Top with coarsely chopped nuts or an icing.
  Excellent choices include Caramel Cream
  Cheese (page 81), Caramel Cream (page 81)
  or Lemon Butter Icing (page 81).

GOOSEBERRY CAKE

Serves 10–12

A rich, rewarding cake with a most unusual flavour. Serve plain or with whipped cream, as a cake or dessert. Use any diced raw fruit, such as grapes, apples, peaches, pears or a combination of these, instead of gooseberries.

100 g (100 ml) butter or hard
  margarine, softened
150 g (175 ml) castor sugar
50 ml olive oil
2 eggs
5 ml vanilla essence
180 g (375 ml) Golden Cloud cake flour
5 ml baking powder
2 ml salt
2 ml bicarbonate of soda
125 ml hanepoot wine
125 ml water
250 ml halved gooseberries
  (fresh or tinned)

TOPPING

30 ml butter or hard margarine
30 ml sugar

1 Preheat the oven to 200°C. Grease a 22 cm pie dish or springform cake tin.
2 Beat together the butter or margarine and castor sugar in a food processor, or with an electric mixer, until creamy. Add the oil, eggs and vanilla essence, and beat until combined.
3 Add the flour, baking powder, salt and bicarb, and beat in. Add the wine and water, and beat until blended. Transfer the mixture to the prepared pie dish or tin. Smooth the top and scatter gooseberries on top.
4 Place into the oven, reduce the oven temperature to 180°C, and bake for 20 minutes, until the cake is just firm. Dot the top with butter, sprinkle with sugar and bake 20 minutes more.
5 Allow the cake to cool in the dish for 20 minutes before serving, or in the tin for 10 minutes before removing. Serve slightly warm or cool.

STAINED-GLASS FRUITCAKE

Serves about 30

A stunning festive cake that tastes as good as it looks.

150 g pecan nuts
100 g red glacé cherries (whole)
100 g green glacé cherries (whole)
200 g (300 ml) chopped glacé fruit
  (e.g. pineapple and apricots)
100 g brazil nuts
3 eggs
50 g (125 ml) castor sugar
5 ml vanilla essence
50 ml brandy or rum
85 g (175 ml) Golden Cloud cake flour
2 ml baking powder
5 ml mixed spice, or ground cardamom
1 ml salt
50 g (50 ml) butter or hard margarine,
  softened

GARNISH

smooth apricot jam or marmalade
whole nuts and fruit for decorating

1 Preheat the oven to 150°C. Line a medium (26 cm) loaf tin with baking paper or greaseproof paper. Grease the paper.
2 Mix together the fruit and nuts in a bowl. Beat together the eggs, castor sugar, vanilla essence and brandy or rum in a food processor, or with an electric mixer. Mix together the flour, baking powder, mixed spice or cardamom and salt, and add to the egg mixture. Add the butter or margarine, and the fruit and nuts to the egg mixture. Stir well to blend evenly. Spoon into the prepared tin, smooth the top and cover with greased foil.
3 Bake for 2 hours, until the cake is firm and a cake-tester comes out clean. Allow the cake to cool in the tin. Turn out and wrap in foil.
4 When ready to serve, warm the jam and brush onto the cake. Decorate with nuts and fruit. Glaze the nuts and fruit with jam as well. Slice thinly or cut into fingers to serve.

COOK'S NOTE
Bake in smaller loaf tins or small cake tins and wrap in cellophane as a gift.

ICINGS, FILLINGS & SAUCES

Specific icings, fillings, frostings and toppings
are included in the recipes in this book, but it is always
fun to ring in the changes. Here are some wonderful
ideas to mix and match, or to swap for
a change of pace.

SWEETENED WHIPPED CREAM

Makes about 375 ml

250 ml cream (well chilled)
15–30 ml sugar
1–2 drops vanilla essence (optional)

1 Place the cream and sugar into a mixing bowl, and beat at moderate speed until stiff and fluffy. Beat in the vanilla essence (if using). Don't overbeat cream, or attempt to beat cream that is slightly warm, otherwise it will separate.
2 Whipped cream can be stored for several hours in the refrigerator. Seal well, as it absorbs odours easily. Whipped cream for filling or garnishing freezes well, and cream rosettes can be frozen and stored in airtight containers. Use directly from the freezer; they thaw quickly.

WHIPPED CREAM VARIATIONS

Boozy Whipped Cream
Add 15–30 ml brandy, rum or liqueur of your choice to the cream before whipping. Sweeten to taste with castor sugar.
Chocolate Whipped Cream
Sift together 15–30 ml cocoa powder and 15–30 ml icing sugar, and add to the cream before whipping.
Mocha-Coffee Whipped Cream
Add 10 ml instant coffee powder to the Chocolate Whipped Cream, or use only coffee. Flavour with Kahlúa liqueur or vanilla essence.
Milo Whipped Cream
Add 50 ml Milo before whipping the cream.

MASCARPONE CHEESE FILLING

Makes about 500 ml

500 g mascarpone cheese, or half mascarpone, half ricotta cheese
50 g (100 ml) icing sugar
few drops vanilla essence or lemon juice

Beat the ingredients to obtain a thick, spreading consistency.

CHOCOLATE GLAZE

Makes about 300 ml

150 g dark chocolate (or half dark, half milk chocolate)
100 ml cream
2 ml vanilla essence
50 g (100 ml) icing sugar

Melt the chocolate (see page 11). Gently stir in the cream and vanilla essence. Sift in the icing sugar, and beat until smooth and shiny. Spread the glaze onto the cake and refrigerate for several hours to firm up before serving.

CHOCOLATE SOUR CREAM GLAZE

Makes about 200 ml

150 g dark or milk chocolate, or use half of each
125 ml sour cream

Melt the chocolate (see page 11). Add the sour cream and beat well with a spoon until blended. Cool for a few minutes and spread onto the cake. The soft glaze will set when the cake is refrigerated.

COCOA SOUR CREAM GLAZE

Makes about 250 ml

200 g (400 ml) icing sugar, sifted
50 ml cocoa powder
50 ml sour cream (approximate amount)
5 ml vanilla essence

Place the icing sugar and cocoa into a mixing bowl. Add the sour cream and vanilla essence. Beat well with a spoon until smooth and thick. Add a little extra sour cream if necessary for a spreading consistency. The glaze is soft but will set when the cake is refrigerated.

CHOCOLATE BUTTER ICING

Makes about 250 ml

50 ml cocoa powder
50 ml boiling water
100 g (100 ml) butter or hard
  margarine, cut into cubes and
  softened
5 ml vanilla essence
200 g (400 ml) icing sugar, sifted

Mix together the cocoa and boiling water
in a cup and stir until smooth. Place the
butter or margarine, vanilla essence and
icing sugar into a mixing bowl and add
the cocoa, beating constantly until fluffy.
Add a little extra icing sugar if necessary
for a spreading consistency.

CHOCOLATE FUDGE ICING

Makes about 250 ml

50 g (50 ml) butter or hard margarine,
  softened
50 ml sour cream, creamed cottage
  cheese or buttermilk
200 g (400 ml) icing sugar, sifted
  (approximate amount)
50 ml cocoa powder
5 ml vanilla essence

Place the butter or margarine and sour
cream, cottage cheese or buttermilk into
a mixing bowl, and mix lightly with a spoon
(don't use an electric beater). Add the icing
sugar, cocoa and vanilla essence, and
continue to beat until smooth and fudge-
like. Add a little extra icing sugar if necessary
for a spreading consistency.

CARAMEL CREAM

Makes about 250 ml sauce (topping)
or 375 ml cream (filling)

250 ml fresh or long-life cream,
50 g (60 ml) brown sugar
2 ml vanilla essence

1 Place the cream and brown sugar into a
  medium saucepan and bring to the boil,
  stirring. Reduce the heat and simmer very
  gently for 10 minutes. Stir in the vanilla
  essence. Pour into a bowl large enough for
  whipping. Cover and refrigerate for at least
  3 hours or overnight, until well chilled.
2 If a pouring sauce is required, beat lightly
  with a whisk. If caramel cream is required,
  beat until stiff and fill or ice the cake. The
  boiled cream, whipped cream, or completed
  cake can be refrigerated for up to 4 days.
3 The mixture will be thick enough for piping
  rosettes, borders, etc. Pipe onto baking trays,
  freeze and store in an airtight container. Use
  from the freezer, they thaw quickly.

CARAMEL CREAM VARIATIONS

Caramel Cream Cheese
Whip the Caramel Cream until stiff and beat
in 125 g (125 ml) firm cream cheese and
5–10 ml lemon juice to create a thick, creamy
filling or topping. Double the cream cheese
for a more pronounced cheese flavour. This
icing is perfect for Golden Carrot Cake
(page 66) and any chocolate or sponge cake.
Chocolate Caramel Cream
Coarsely chop 100 g dark or white chocolate,
add to the hot caramel cream and stir until
the chocolate has melted. Chill thoroughly
before whipping. Use with either Caramel
Cream or the Caramel Cream Cheese
variation. Excellent for filling and garnishing
chocolate cake or plain sponge cake.
Coffee Caramel Cream
Add 15–30 ml Kahlúa liqueur or 5 ml vanilla
essence, and 10 ml instant coffee powder to
the hot Caramel Cream or Caramel Cream
Cheese. Stir well and chill.

BUTTER ICING

Sufficient to fill and top 1 medium cake

*A versatile, basic icing that is quick
to make.*

60 g (60 ml) butter or hard margarine,
  softened
130 g (250 ml) icing sugar, sifted
few drops milk, cream or water
2 ml vanilla essence

1 Place the butter or margarine and icing
  sugar into a mixing bowl, or the bowl of
  a food processor, and beat or process until
  well combined.
2 Add the milk, cream or water, a few drops
  at a time, while beating or processing to
  a spreading consistency. Beat in the
  vanilla essence.
3 Adjust the consistency if necessary by adding
  a few extra drops of liquid or a little extra
  icing sugar. Refrigerate until required, but
  bring to room temperature before spreading.

BUTTER ICING VARIATIONS

Chocolate Butter Icing
Add 15 ml cocoa powder to the icing sugar,
and an additional 2 ml vanilla essence.
Coffee Butter Icing
Dissolve 10–15 ml instant coffee granules
in 15 ml hot water, and add to the mixture.
A few drops of Kahlúa liqueur can be added
instead of or with the vanilla essence.
Almond Butter Icing
Add 2 ml almond essence when adding
the vanilla essence.
Lemon Butter Icing
Add to the mixture 15 ml lemon juice, and
up to 30 ml finely grated lemon zest.
Granadilla Butter Icing
Add the pulp of 3 fresh granadillas and 5 ml
lemon juice to the bowl with the icing sugar,
or use 30 ml strained, tinned granadilla pulp.
Coloured / Flavoured Butter Icing
Add a (very) few drops food colouring, or
essences such as caramel or banana. Use
corresponding colour and flavouring such as
egg yellow colouring with banana essence.

BUTTER CREAM

Makes about 500 ml

Watchpoint: the success of Butter Cream lies in the mixing, so follow the method strictly.

150 g (175 ml) sugar
pinch cream of tartar
80 ml water
5 egg yolks
200 g (225 ml) butter or hard
   margarine, cut into blocks and
   softened
extra butter or hard margarine, if needed
7 ml vanilla essence

1 Place the sugar, cream of tartar and water into a saucepan, and stir over low heat until the sugar is completely dissolved. Boil the syrup without stirring, until soft ball stage is reached (a syrup thermometer should register 114°C or, 238°F or the syrup would have reduced by about one-third and a few drops in cold water will form a soft ball). Watchpoint: if the syrup is not boiled to the right stage no amount of beating will correct the butter cream. If the syrup is boiled for too long it will form crystals or lumps in the beaten egg.
2 While the syrup is boiling, beat the egg yolks until light and fluffy. Pour the hot syrup into the egg in a very thin stream, beating constantly. Continue beating while the mixture cools, until it becomes a thick, light mousse. Allow to cool to room temperature.
3 Slowly add the butter or margarine bit by bit, beating constantly to a thick emulsion. Add a little extra butter or margarine if necessary to firm the butter cream. Beat in the vanilla essence.
4 Use immediately or refrigerate until required. Remove from the fridge before spreading to soften slightly. Note: butter cream can be refrigerated in a sealed container for up to 2 weeks. It may also be frozen as part of a completed cake.

BUTTER CREAM VARIATIONS

Chocolate Butter Cream
Add 60 ml cocoa powder to the syrup before pouring into the egg. Or, melt 100 g dark chocolate (see page 11) and beat in with 30–60 ml brandy.

Nut and Rum Butter Cream
Place 100 g finely ground walnuts, almonds or hazels into a bowl and stir in 50 ml rum. Beat well into the Butter Cream. Substitute brandy or Amaretto for the rum.

Coffee-Mocha Butter Cream
Place 50 ml instant coffee granules into a bowl and stir in 30–60 ml brandy. Melt 50–100 g dark chocolate (see page 11). Allow to cool. Beat the coffee and chocolate into the finished Butter Cream.

Almond Butter Cream
Beat in 5 ml almond essence with the vanilla essence.

MILK-BASED BUTTER CREAM VARIATIONS

Chocolate Milk-based Butter Cream
Break 100–200 g dark chocolate into the warming milk. Heat gently, stirring until dissolved. Complete the recipe.

Mocha Milk-based Butter Cream
Add 80 ml cocoa powder and 30 ml instant coffee granules to the milk before heating it. A little brandy, rum, Kahlúa liqueur or other chocolate or coffee-based liqueur is also nice. Or add coffee granules to the recipe for Chocolate Butter Cream.

Almond Milk-based Butter Cream
Increase the almond essence to l0 ml, and decorate the completed cake with roasted flaked or nibbed almonds (see page 12).

MILK-BASED BUTTER CREAM

Sufficient for 1 large cake

500 ml milk
60 ml cornflour
100 g (125 ml) sugar
5 ml vanilla essence
2 ml almond essence
200–250 g (225–280 ml) butter
   or hard margarine, cut into small
   cubes and softened
extra butter or hard margarine, if needed

1 Pour 400 ml of the milk into a medium saucepan and bring to the boil. Mix together the cornflour and remaining milk, and pour into the milk, stirring constantly until it boils and thickens. Stir in the sugar and essences, and simmer for 1 minute. To cook in the microwave, place the milk, cornflour and sugar into a bowl and beat well. Microwave on High for 2 minutes. Beat with a whisk. Microwave for 2 minutes. Beat well. Microwave for 1 minute until the mixture becomes thick, smooth and shiny. Pour the sauce into the bowl of an electric mixer and allow to cool to room temperature.
2 Ensure that the sauce and the butter or margarine are at room temperature (soft but not melted), before continuing otherwise you won't be able to form an emulsion, and the butter cream may separate or curdle.
3 Beat the sauce to lighten it. Beat in the butter or margarine bit by bit, beating well after each addition. Continue beating to a smooth, thick emulsion. If necessary, beat in a little extra butter or margarine. Refrigerate for at least 30 minutes. Note: If the butter cream separates, place an egg yolk into a clean bowl and beat in teaspoonfuls of the butter cream at a time, until the emulsion is restored. Beat in the remaining butter cream a tablespoon at a time. Note: Flavour this recipe in any of the ways suggested for Butter Cream Variations alongside.

EGG-YOLK BUTTER ICING

Makes about 200 ml

130 g (250 ml) icing sugar
30 ml butter or hard margarine,
    softened
1 egg yolk
5 ml vanilla essence
a few drops milk

Place the icing sugar, butter or margarine,
egg yolk and vanilla essence into a mixing
bowl, and beat well. Add a few drops of milk
if the mixture is too dry, and beat until the
icing becomes light and fluffy.

MERINGUE BUTTER CREAM

Makes about 500 ml

125 ml water
15 ml golden syrup
200 g (250 ml) sugar
3 egg whites
200 g (225 ml) butter or hard
    margarine, cubed and softened

1 Place the water and syrup into a medium
  saucepan, together with two-thirds of the
  sugar. Stir over low heat until the sugar has
  melted. Boil without stirring, until the syrup
  reaches soft ball stage (it will have reduced
  by one-third, a few drops in cold water will
  form a soft ball and a syrup thermometer
  will register 114°C (238°F).
2 Meanwhile, beat the egg whites until soft
  peaks form. Gradually beat in the remaining
  sugar until stiff and glossy.
3 Pour the syrup into the egg white in a thin
  stream, beating constantly until smooth and
  stiff. Set aside to cool. Beat in the butter or
  margarine bit by bit until thick and light.
  Meringue Butter Cream can be refrigerated
  a for up to a week.

EGG-YOLK BUTTER ICING VARIATIONS

Chocolate Egg-yolk Butter Icing
Add 30 ml cocoa powder.
Citrus Egg-yolk Butter Icing
Add grated orange or lemon zest.
Almond Egg-yolk Butter Icing
Add a drop or two of almond essence
or a little Amaretto or Frangelico liqueur.

TINNED FRUIT SAUCE

Makes about 600 ml

410 g tin fruit (stoned cherries,
    any berries, apricots)
30 ml cornflour
250 ml water
1 stick cinnamon (optional)
30–60 ml sugar

1 Prepare the fruit any way you wish:
  leave whole, cut into chunks, or purée
  in a food processor or blender with the
  syrup from the tin. Strain through a sieve
  for extra smoothness.
2 Place the fruit (with the syrup from the tin),
  whole, chopped or puréed, into a saucepan
  with the cinnamon (if using). Mix together
  the cornflour and water and stir into the
  sauce. Bring to boil, stirring constantly, until
  the sauce is smooth and clear.
3 Add sugar to taste; simmer for 1–2 minutes
  more. Discard the cinnamon. Serve chilled,
  cool or warm as required. The sauce can be
  refrigerated for up to two weeks.

FRESH FRUIT SAUCE

Makes about 500 ml

500 g fresh fruit (strawberries, plums,
    apricots, mangoes)
10 ml cornflour
50 ml water
50–125 ml sugar

1 Wash and prepare the fruit. Hull
  strawberries; stone plums and apricots; peel
  and stone mangoes. Cut into neat portions.
2 Place the fruit into a medium saucepan with
  the cornflour and water and bring to the
  boil, stirring constantly. Simmer for a couple
  of minutes until the fruit is tender. Add
  sugar to taste, taking into account the
  sweetness or acidity of the fruit, and simmer
  for a few minutes more.
3 Serve the sauce chunky, or puréed smoothly
  in a food processor or blender.

FRESH FRUIT PURÉES

Purée fresh fruit such as strawberries, melons,
kiwi fruit, mangoes or pineapple; sweeten
and use within a few hours.

FRUIT TOPPINGS

1 Cover cakes just before serving with fresh,
  sliced fruit such as strawberries, kiwi fruit,
  mangoes, or any fruit that will not discolour
  too quickly after slicing. Note: to reduce
  discolouring dip the fruit in a mixture of
  15 ml lemon juice, 15 ml castor sugar and
  125 ml water.
2 Use 15 ml gelatine per 500 ml of any fruit
  sauce, except for pineapple, which does not
  set with gelatine. Place the gelatine into a
  jug, add enough of the fruit sauce to cover
  well and melt over simmering water, or
  microwave on Medium for about 1 minute.
  Stir the melted gelatine back into the
  remaining fruit sauce and refrigerate until it
  starts to set. Spoon onto the cake or pie, and
  refrigerate for at least 1 hour until firm.

YEAST BREADS
BREAD & ROLLS

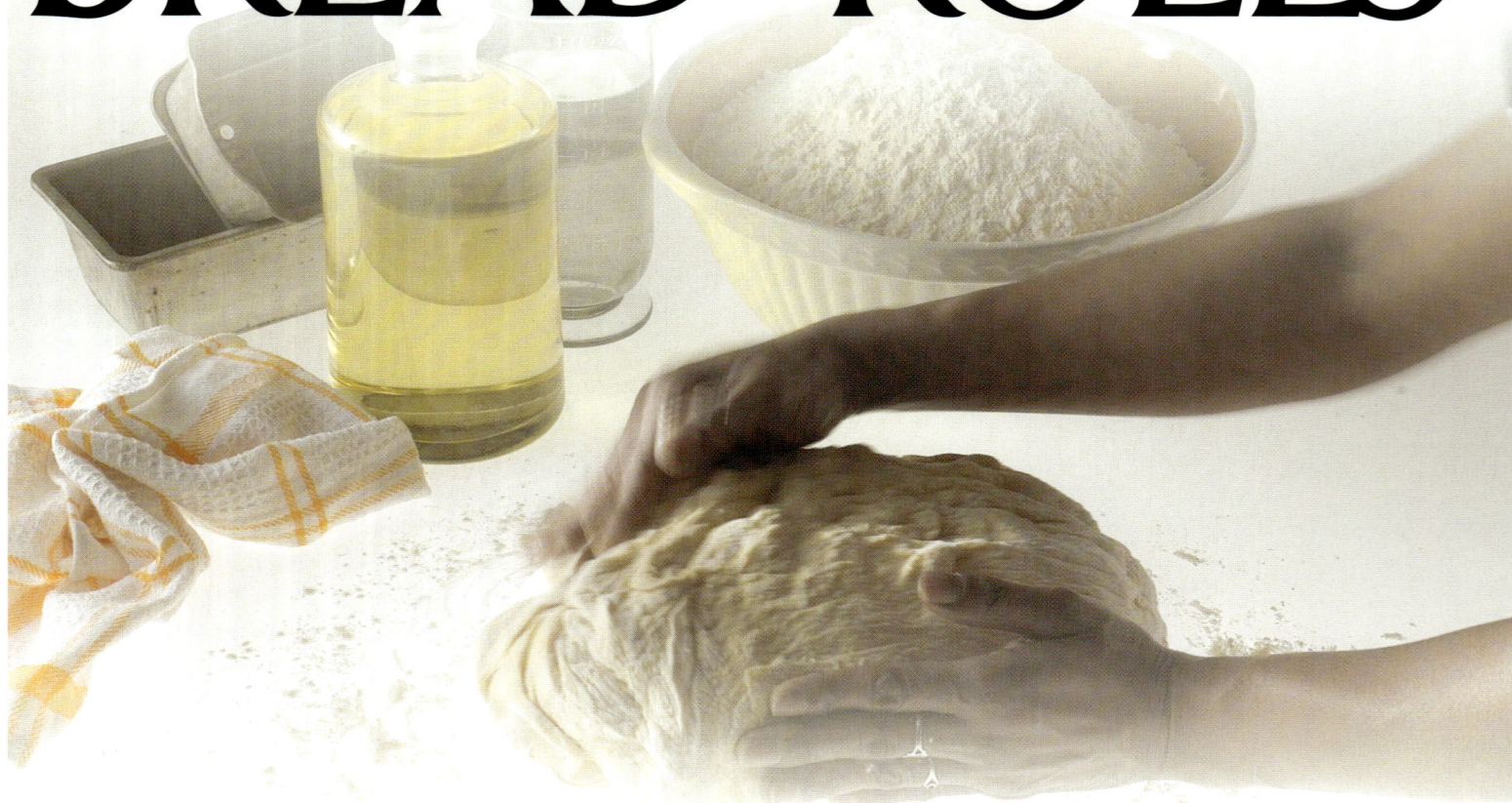

There's nothing quite like the aroma of baking bread wafting through the house, nor the satisfaction of slicing a crusty, oven-warm loaf that you have baked yourself.

If your baking repertoire has thus far only extended to cakes and biscuits, yeast breads and rolls will introduce you to a new world of pleasures. Discover other types of flour, such as white and brown bread flour, and coarsely textured wholewheat flour. Feel the grainy taste of nature, as you add semolina, maize meal, cheese, fruit and crunchy seeds to the breads. Best of all, you will know the satisfaction of kneading dough with your own hands, and marvelling as the yeast does its amazing thing, and the dough rises and takes shape.

All sorts of breads are included here, from feather-light to chewy; silky fine to crumbly and coarse. Contemporary and classic recipes alike will introduce you to a world of culinary pleasures, be you a novice or experienced baker. Contrary to the perception that baking with yeast is an acquired skill, you'll find it simple and straightforward. It is, however, a good idea to first study techniques for Yeast Baking on page 12. For perfect results, always use the type of flour specified in the recipe.

All the loaves in this chapter can be divided to make mini loaves: spoon the dough into well-greased mini loaf tins or 200–250 ml muffin cups, filling them to no more than two-thirds full. Adjust the rising and baking times accordingly.

Focaccia page 87

Rye Bread page 88

Bread Rolls page 97

RICH WHITE BREAD

Makes 2 large loaves

This dough makes wonderful bread rolls too. The oil ensures good keeping quality, especially if the bread is made with one sachet of yeast and allowed to rise slowly.

1–2 x 10 g sachets instant yeast
   (quantity depends on available time)
360 g (750 ml) Golden Cloud cake flour
625 ml lukewarm water
1 egg
125 ml sunflower oil
30 ml sugar
12 ml salt
500 g (1 litre) extra Golden Cloud
   cake flour
GLAZE
1 egg
50 ml water

1 Generously grease two 28 cm loaf tins.
2 Place the yeast and the first measure of flour into a mixing bowl, or the bowl of an electric mixer fitted with the dough hook. Add all the remaining ingredients – except the extra flour – and mix well.
3 Gradually add enough of the extra flour to form a soft dough. Knead for 5–6 minutes (with the electric mixer), or turn out onto a floured surface and knead by hand for 6–8 minutes, until smooth and elastic. Shape into a ball, and return the dough to the mixing bowl. Cover, and allow to rise for about 45 minutes, until doubled in bulk.
4 Punch down the dough and divide in half. Shape into neat loaves and place into the prepared tins. For more professional loaves, roll each portion out onto an oiled surface to a thickness of about 15 mm, and as wide and as long as the tin. Roll up neatly, tuck the ends under and place into the tin, seam down. The tins should be about half full. Shape any excess dough into bread rolls (page 97).
5 Set aside, uncovered, until the dough has doubled in bulk, and rises above the edge of the tins. Meanwhile, preheat the oven to 170°C.
6 Mix together the egg and water to make the glaze, and brush over the top of the bread. Bake for about 45 minutes, until the loaves sound hollow when tapped, and the crust is golden brown. Allow to cool for a few minutes in the tins, then shake and turn out onto a wire rack to cool completely.

RICH WHITE BREAD VARIATION

Light Brown Bread
Replace between two-thirds and half the cake flour with Golden Cloud Krakley Wheat wholewheat flour, and increase the salt to 15 ml.

WHITE BREAD

Makes 1 large loaf

This dough is a useful base for many variations as described in recipes that follow.

10 g sachet instant yeast
240 g (500 ml) Golden Cloud cake flour
375 ml lukewarm water
50 ml sunflower oil
10 ml sugar
5 ml salt
120 g (250 ml) extra cake flour
   (approximate amount)

1 Generously grease one 28 cm loaf tin.
2 Place the yeast and the first measure of flour into a mixing bowl or the bowl of an electric mixer fitted with the dough hook. Add all the remaining ingredients – except the extra flour – and mix well.
3 Gradually add enough of the extra flour to form a soft dough. Knead for 4–5 minutes (with the mixer), or turn out onto a floured surface and knead by hand for about 5 minutes, until smooth and elastic. Sprinkle the dough lightly with flour and shape into a neat ball. Return the dough to the bowl, cover and set aside in a warm spot to rise for about 40 minutes, until doubled in bulk.
4 Punch down the dough, shape neatly and place into the prepared tin. Set aside, uncovered, until doubled again in bulk. Meanwhile preheat the oven to 170°C.
5 Bake for about 45 minutes, until the loaf sounds hollow when tapped, and the crust is golden brown. Allow to cool for a few minutes in the tin, then cool on a wire rack.

COOK'S NOTES
- For a more chewy bread, use white bread flour instead of cake flour.
- To make brown bread, substitute half the flour with Golden Cloud Krakley Wheat wholewheat flour, or Golden Cloud brown bread flour.

FOCACCIA

Makes 8–12 flatbreads, depending on size

Mediterranean flatbread is great with cheese, pâté, pasta, soup or salad.

White Bread dough (page 86)
15 ml fresh rosemary needles
olive oil for brushing
extra rosemary sprigs and coarse salt
  for sprinkling

1 Grease two medium baking trays.
2 Prepare the white bread dough, following
  steps 1–3. Punch down and knead in the
  fresh rosemary needles.
3 Pinch off apple-sized balls and roll out into
  flattish ovals about 15–20 mm thick. Place
  onto the baking trays. Cut slits to resemble
  a leaf pattern (two on each side in the shape
  of a 'V'; one downwards in the centre of
  the top 'V')
4 Brush with olive oil, sprinkle with coarse salt,
  and stick in rosemary sprigs. Allow to rise
  until almost doubled in bulk. Meanwhile
  preheat the oven to 200°C.
5 Bake for about 15 minutes until the
  focaccias are crisp and golden. Place onto
  a wire rack and allow to cool.
6 Serve with butter, or olive oil and balsamic
  vinegar for dipping, if preferred.

> ## COOK'S NOTES
> • Make two large focaccias instead
>   of smaller ones.
> • Knead chopped olives and/or sun-dried
>   tomatoes into the dough for added flavour.

> ## COOK'S NOTE
> Experiment with various fillings, such as ham,
> mushrooms, asparagus or tuna, either
> together with, or instead of, the vegetables.

FILLED FOCACCIA

Makes 2 filled flatbreads; 16 wedges

Split and fill flatbreads to serve as a light meal, or to accompany a braai.

White Bread dough (page 86)
coarse salt
sprigs of fresh rosemary (optional)
VEGETABLE AND CHEESE FILLING
200 g courgettes, finely diced
1 large red pepper, seeded and diced
30 ml olive oil
100 ml finely chopped spring onions
15 ml chopped fresh herbs,
  or 2 ml mixed dried herbs
salt and milled black pepper
50 g (125 ml) grated cheddar or
  pecorino cheese
100 g (250 ml) grated mozzarella cheese

1 Grease two pizza trays or baking trays.
2 Prepare the dough, following steps 1–3.
  Punch down and divide into two portions.

Press evenly onto the pizza trays, or shape
into rounds and place onto the baking trays.
Sprinkle with coarse salt and stick in the
rosemary sprigs, if using. Set aside for
15–20 minutes, until risen. Meanwhile,
preheat the oven to 180°C.
3 Bake for 20 minutes until the focaccias are
  very pale golden and firm. Lift onto wire
  racks and allow to cool
4 To make the filling, in a large frying pan,
  fry the courgettes and pepper in the oil until
  limp. Add the spring onions and herbs, and
  season with salt and pepper. Cook for about
  5 minutes. Allow to cool to room
  temperature, then mix in the cheeses.
5 Cut the focaccias in half horizontally, and
  fill with the vegetable mixture. Wrap in
  foil for at least 1 hour (up to two days
  in the fridge).
6 About 45 minutes before serving, preheat
  the oven to 180°C. Place the foil-wrapped
  focaccias onto baking trays, and bake for
  25 minutes. Open the foil and bake for
  5 minutes more. Cut into wedges; Serve hot.

HERBED WHITE BREAD WITH SUN-DRIED TOMATOES

Makes 1 large loaf

720 g (1.5 litres / 6 x 250 ml cups)
Golden Cloud white bread flour
1–2 x 10 g sachets instant yeast
(quantity depends on available time)
10 ml sugar
10 ml salt
600 ml lukewarm water
extra water and flour (optional)
60 ml sunflower oil
60 ml chopped, sun-dried tomatoes
30 ml chopped, fresh basil
30 ml chopped, fresh oregano
milled black pepper

1 Generously grease a 28 cm loaf tin.
2 Place the flour, yeast, sugar and salt into a mixing bowl, or the bowl of an electric mixer fitted with the dough hook. Add the water and oil. Mix to a heavy batter; it should be quite firm but not stiff enough to knead. If necessary add a little extra water or flour. Mix for about 2 minutes until just sticky.
3 Add the sun-dried tomatoes and the herbs, and mix to combine evenly. Spoon the batter into the prepared tin. Sprinkle with black pepper. Set aside to rise, uncovered, until well rounded on top; this will take about 20 minutes if 2 sachets of yeast have been used; 40 minutes if one sachet has been used. Meanwhile, preheat the oven to 200°C.
4 Bake the bread for about 45 minutes until the crust is browned, the loaf sounds hollow when tapped, and a cake-tester comes out clean. Turn out onto a wire rack to cool.

COOK'S NOTES
• Replace the sun-dried tomatoes with stoned, chopped calamata olives, or use half sun-dried tomatoes, half olives.
• To make cheese bread add to the batter 100–200 g (250–500 ml) coarsely grated cheddar cheese.

SEMOLINA BREAD

Makes 1 medium loaf

Semolina adds a creamy colour and rich, nutty flavour to bread, making this one of the most delicious white loaves in the book.

10 g sachet instant yeast
200 g (250 ml) Golden Cloud semolina
280 g (500 ml) Golden Cloud white
bread flour, or 240 g (500 ml)
Golden Cloud cake flour
15 ml sugar
7 ml salt
375 ml lukewarm water
30 ml olive or sunflower oil
140 g (250 ml) extra Golden Cloud
white bread flour, or 120 g (250 ml)
Golden Cloud cake flour (approximate
amount)
1 egg white for brushing
sesame or poppy seeds for sprinkling
(optional)

1 Grease a 26 cm loaf tin.
2 Place the yeast, semolina, flour, sugar and salt into a mixing bowl, or the bowl of an electric mixer fitted with the dough hook. Mix thoroughly. Mix in the water and oil.
3 Gradually add extra flour to form a soft dough. Knead for 5 minutes (with the electric mixer), or turn out onto a floured surface and knead for 6–8 minutes by hand, until smooth and elastic. Return the dough to the bowl, cover, and set aside for about 45 minutes, until doubled in bulk.
4 Punch the dough down and shape into a neat roll to fit the tin, making it just more than half full. Brush with unbeaten egg white and sprinkle with seeds, if used. Allow to rise, uncovered, until the top is well rounded. Preheat the oven to 190°C.
5 Bake for about 35 minutes, until the loaf sounds hollow when tapped, and the crust is browned. Allow to cool in the tin for a short while, then turn out onto a wire rack to cool completely.

RYE BREAD

Makes 2 medium loaves

Excellent with soup, or cold meats, cheeses and salad.

240 g (500 ml) rye flour
120 g (250 ml) Golden Cloud cake flour
10 g sachet instant yeast
15 ml brown sugar
10 ml salt
5–10 ml caraway seeds (optional)
30 g (30 ml) butter, hard margarine
or sunflower oil
400 ml lukewarm water
20 ml honey, treacle or molasses
120 g (250 ml) extra Golden Cloud cake
flour (approximate amount)

1 Grease a baking tray. Place the rye flour, first measure of cake flour, yeast, brown sugar, salt and caraway seeds into a mixing bowl or the bowl of an electric mixer fitted with the dough hook. Mix to combine. Add the butter, margarine or oil, water, and honey and/or treacle or molasses and mix well.
2 Add sufficient of the remaining flour to form a soft, kneadable dough that is not too sticky. Knead for 3–4 minutes with the electric mixer, or turn out onto a floured surface, and knead by hand for 5 minutes. Return the dough to the bowl, cover and set aside for 15 minutes. Knock down, cover and set aside for 15 minutes more. Meanwhile preheat the oven to 200°C.
3 Divide the dough in half and shape into ovals. Place onto the baking tray, and slash the tops with a sharp knife. Sprinkle lightly with rye flour and allow to rise, uncovered, until doubled in bulk.
4 Place the loaves in the oven, reduce the temperature to 190°C and bake for 15 minutes. Reduce the temperature to 180°C and bake for 15–20 minutes more until they sound hollow when tapped, and the crusts are golden brown. Place on a wire rack and allow to cool.

ANADAMA BREAD

Makes one medium loaf

*An enticing, aromatic South American bread
with an interesting texture.*

10 g sachet instant yeast
60 g (125 ml) Ace Super maize meal
100 g (125 ml) Golden Cloud semolina
375 ml lukewarm water
60 g (50 ml) molasses
50 g (50 ml) butter or hard margarine,
    cut into cubes and softened
7 ml salt
280 g (500 ml) Golden Cloud white
    bread flour, or 240 g (500 ml)
    Golden Cloud cake flour
140 g (250 ml) extra Golden Cloud
    white bread flour, or 120 g (250 ml)
    Golden Cloud cake flour
1 egg white for brushing
sesame or poppy seeds for sprinkling

1 Grease a 26 cm loaf tin.
2 Place the yeast, maize meal and semolina
  into a mixing bowl, or the bowl of an electric
  mixer fitted with the dough hook. Mix
  thoroughly. Add the water, molasses, butter
  or margarine, salt and first measure of flour,
  and mix until combined.
3 Gradually add extra flour to form a soft
  dough. Knead for 5 minutes (with the
  electric mixer), or turn out onto a floured
  surface and knead by hand for 6–8 minutes,
  until smooth and elastic. Return the dough
  to the bowl, cover, and set aside to rise for
  about 45 minutes, until doubled in bulk.
4 Punch down the dough, and shape into a
  neat roll to fit the tin, making it a little more
  than half full. Brush with unbeaten egg
  white and sprinkle with seeds. Allow to rise,
  uncovered, until the top is well rounded.
  Meanwhile preheat the oven to 190°C.
5 Bake for about 35 minutes, until the loaf
  sounds hollow when tapped, and the crust is
  browned. Allow to cool in the tin for a short
  while, then turn out onto a wire rack to cool.

ANADAMA BREAD VARIATIONS

Light Brown Anadama Bread
Replace half the bread or cake flour with
Golden Cloud Krakley Wheat wholewheat
flour, and sprinkle crushed wheat on top of
the dough before baking the bread.

LIGHT BROWN
SEED BREAD VARIATION

Light Brown Nutty Prune Bread
Add to the batter 10 stoned, halved prunes,
and 50 ml coarsely chopped pecan nuts
or mixed nuts.

LIGHT BROWN SEED BREAD

Makes 1 large loaf

Even novice bread bakers can manage this delicious, quick-to-make recipe. For smaller loaves, bake in two 23 cm loaf tins.

poppy, sesame and sunflower seeds for
  sprinkling
850 g (1.5 litres / 6 x 250 ml cups)
  Golden Cloud brown bread flour
1–2 x 10 g sachets instant yeast
  (quantity depends on available time)
10 ml sugar
10 ml salt
50 ml sesame seeds
50 ml poppy seeds
600 ml lukewarm water
60 ml sunflower oil
extra water or flour, if necessary

1 Generously grease a 28 cm loaf tin. Sprinkle lightly with seeds.
2 Place the flour, yeast, sugar, salt and seeds into a bowl, or the bowl of an electric mixer fitted with the dough hook. Add the water and oil. Mix to a heavy batter; it should be quite firm, but not stiff enough to knead. If necessary, add a little extra water or flour. Mix for about 2 minutes, just until sticky.
3 Spoon the batter into the prepared tin. Sprinkle with sunflower seeds. Set aside to rise, uncovered, until well rounded on top. This will take about 20 minutes if 2 sachets of yeast have been used; about 40 minutes if 1 sachet has been used. Meanwhile preheat the oven to 200°C.
4 Bake for about 45 minutes, until the crust is browned, the loaf sounds hollow when tapped, and a cake-tester comes out clean. Turn out onto a wire rack and allow to cool.

SUPER GRAIN BREAD

Makes 2 medium loaves

A grainy, textured loaf. This dough makes super fancy-shaped bread rolls.

60 g (125 ml) Ace Super maize meal
50 g (60 ml) brown sugar
60 ml sunflower oil
375 ml boiling water
250 ml cold water
10 g sachet instant yeast
15 ml salt
175 g (375 ml) rye flour
100 ml digestive bran or wheat germ
240 g (500 ml) Golden Cloud cake flour,
  or 280 g (500 ml) Golden Cloud
  white or brown bread flour
350 g (750 ml) extra Golden Cloud cake
  flour, or 420 g (750 ml) Golden
  Cloud white or brown bread flour
  (approximate amount)

1 Grease two 26 cm loaf tins.
2 Place the maize meal, sugar, oil and boiling water into a mixing bowl, or the bowl of an electric mixer fitted with the dough hook. Mix well. Allow to stand for a few minutes. Add the cold water, and all the remaining ingredients – except the extra flour – and mix again.
3 Gradually add sufficient of the extra flour to form a soft dough. Knead for 5 minutes (electric mixer), or turn out onto a floured surface and knead by hand for 5–6 minutes, until smooth and elastic. Return the dough to the bowl, cover, and allow to rise for about 40 minutes, until doubled in bulk.
4 Punch down the dough, and divide it in half. Shape into neat loaves, and place into the tins. Allow to rise until the dough is well rounded above the edge of the tins. Meanwhile preheat the oven to 180°C.
5 Bake for about 40 minutes, until the loaves are golden and a cake-tester comes out clean. Allow to cool in the tins for a few minutes, then turn out onto a wire rack.

HEALTH BREAD WITH SEEDS AND BRAN

Makes 2 medium loaves

crushed wheat for sprinkling
    into the tin
480 g (1 litre) Golden Cloud cake flour,
    or 560 g (1 litre) Golden Cloud
    white bread flour
560 g (1 litre) Golden Cloud Krakley
    Wheat wholewheat flour
80 g (500 ml) digestive bran
400 ml seeds (mix sesame seeds,
    sunflower seeds, linseeds and
    poppy seeds)
15 ml salt
2 x 10 g sachets instant yeast
1 litre lukewarm water
125 ml sunflower oil
125 ml honey, or half molasses,
    half honey

1 Generously grease two 26 cm loaf tins.
Sprinkle crushed wheat into the tins. Place
all the bread ingredients into a mixing bowl,
and stir well to make a heavy batter.
2 Spoon into the tins, making them half full,
and smooth the top. Allow to rise uncovered
in a protected spot until filled to the brim.
Meanwhile preheat the oven to 200°C.
3 Bake the bread for 20 minutes. Reduce the
temperature to 180°C and bake for
20 minutes more until the crust is dark
golden brown and firm, and a cake-tester
comes out clean.
4 Allow the bread to cool in the tins for
5 minutes, then turn out onto a wire rack to
cool completely.

COOK'S NOTE
For a seedless loaf omit the seeds and add
200 g (350 ml) extra Golden Cloud Krakley
Wheat wholewheat flour.

HEALTH BREAD WITH ONION AND HERBS

Makes 1 large or 2 smaller loaves

garlic and herb seasoning for sprinkling
    into the tin
200 ml finely chopped onion
    (approximate amount)
1 clove garlic, peeled and crushed,
    or 1 ml garlic and herb seasoning
    50 ml sunflower oil
410 g tin evaporated milk
125 ml water
120 g (250 ml) Ace Super maize meal
280 g (500 ml) Golden Cloud Krakley
    Wheat wholewheat flour
1–2 x 10 g sachets instant yeast
    (quantity depends on available time)
5 ml salt
30 ml sugar
100 ml chopped fresh parsley
2 ml dried dill
2 ml dried sage or oregano
120 g (250 ml) Golden Cloud cake flour
    (approximate amount)

1 Generously grease one 28 cm loaf tin.
Sprinkle with garlic and herb seasoning.
2 Fry the onion and garlic, or garlic and herb
seasoning in the oil in a small saucepan
until the onion is translucent. Remove
from heat and stir in the evaporated milk
and water.
3 Place the maize meal, wholewheat flour,
yeast, salt, sugar, parsley, dill and oregano
into a mixing bowl or the bowl of an
electric mixer fitted with the dough hook.
Mix to combine. Beat in the onion mixture.
4 Add sufficient cake flour to form a soft
dough, and knead for 3–4 minutes until
smooth and elastic. If making by hand:
turn out onto a floured surface and knead
for about 5 minutes. Return the dough to
the bowl. Cover and allow the dough to rise
for about 20 minutes (if 2 sachets of yeast
have been used) or 40 minutes (if one
sachet has been used).
5 Gently punch down the dough. Shape into
rolls, place them into the tin and allow to
rise uncovered until doubled in bulk.
Meanwhile preheat the oven to 180°C.
6 Bake the bread for about 40 minutes until
the crust is browned, the loaf sounds hollow
when tapped, and a cake-tester comes
out clean. Turn out onto a wire rack and
allow to cool.

ROOSTERKOEK

Makes about 20 medium roosterkoek

Crisp, smoky roosterkoek cooked over open coals are a special treat.

White Bread dough (page 86)
sunflower or olive oil

1 Generously grease a medium baking tray with oil. Dust a smooth worktop with flour.
2 Prepare the dough, following steps 1–3. Turn out onto the worktop, and roll out to 20 mm thick. Cut circles with a round 6–8 cm cutter, and place onto the tray. Turn over to coat with oil on all sides.
3 Cover loosely with waxed paper and allow to rise for about 15 minutes at room temperature, or up to 2 hours in the fridge.
4 Arrange the roosterkoek onto a grid and braai over moderately hot coals for 5–8 minutes, until crisp. Turn over and cook the other side.
5 Split the roosterkoek and serve with butter with the meat, or after the braai with jam, honey or syrup.

VETKOEK

Makes 16–20 vetkoek

Fried breads are a South African favourite. To serve, split and fill with jam or honey, grated cheese or savoury meats.

White Bread dough (page 86)
sunflower oil for frying

1 Lightly oil a smooth worktop. Prepare the dough, following steps 1–3. Turn out onto the worktop and roll out to a thickness of about 20 mm. Cut into rounds about 60 mm in diameter. Flatten, gently stretching the dough until it's about 10 mm thick. Set aside to rise until doubled in bulk.
2 Fry one vetkoek at a time in deep oil in a deep saucepan over moderate heat. Immediately stroke the vetkoek with a slotted spoon, and push gently so that it is covered by the oil, until it starts to puff up. This encourages rapid rising in the centre, creating pockets for filling. Turn the vetkoek over and cook until it is golden on the other side. Watchpoint: the temperature of the oil is very important: if it is too cold, the vetkoek will not rise quickly; if it is too hot the vetkoek will brown before they're cooked through.
3 Lift the vetkoek out of the oil with the slotted spoon, and place onto absorbent paper to drain on both sides. Serve warm or cool with a filling of your choice.

KITKE

Makes 2 large loaves

Kitke originated in Israel, and is now baked in homes and bakeries worldwide.

10 g sachet instant yeast
240 g (500 ml) Golden Cloud cake flour
500 ml lukewarm water
50 ml sugar
2 eggs
7 ml salt
60 g (60 ml) butter or hard
  margarine, melted
500 g (1 litre) extra Golden Cloud cake
  flour (approximate amount)
GLAZE
1 egg
15 ml water
sesame or poppy seeds for sprinkling

1 Grease two medium baking trays.
2 Place the yeast and the first measure of flour into a mixing bowl, or the bowl of an electric mixer fitted with the dough hook. Add all the remaining ingredients – except the extra flour – and mix well. Gradually add sufficient of the extra flour to form a soft dough. Knead for 5 minutes (with the electric mixer), or turn out onto a floured surface and knead by hand for 6–8 minutes, until smooth and elastic.
3 Sprinkle the dough with flour, shape into a ball and return it to the bowl. Cover, and set aside to rise, until doubled in bulk.
4 Punch the dough down lightly and divide in half. Set one portion aside.
5 Divide the dough for the first plait in half, making one piece twice as large the other. Divide both portions into 3 balls, so that you end up with 3 large and 3 small balls. Roll the balls out individually under your palms on a lightly floured surface, so that you end up with 6 strands Loosely plait the 3 bigger strands together, and, separately, the 3 smaller ones together, lifting and turning each strand while plaiting to create a bulky, but not flat plait. You will now have one large and one small plait. Lift the small plait and stretch it slightly to fit nicely on top of the larger one. Tuck the ends of the smaller plait underneath the large plait.
6 Repeat the procedure for the second loaf.
7 Beat together the egg and water for the glaze, and brush generously onto the plaits. Place onto the trays, and sprinkle with seeds.
8 Allow the plaits to rise in a protected spot at room temperature, for at least 30 minutes, until doubled in bulk. Watchpoint: if the dough becomes warm, it will lose shape. Meanwhile, preheat the oven to 170°C.
9 Bake for 20–25 minutes until the loaves sound hollow when tapped, and the crusts are golden brown and firm. Place on a wire rack to cool.

KITKE VARIATIONS

Round Kitke Breads
Pack small rolls slightly apart into cake tins.
Glaze and sprinkle with seeds.
Kitke Rolls
Make the dough into rolls (see page 97).
Glaze and add one of the
following toppings:
Seed topping: sprinkle with different seeds
(sesame, poppy, sunflower and linseeds)
before baking.
Cheese Topping: sprinkle 250 ml finely grated
cheddar cheese and Red Sprinkle Mix
(page 12) over the unbaked bread.
Seed and herb mix (Zahter mix): combine
30 ml sesame seeds, 30 ml dried marjoram
or oregano, 10 ml dried thyme, 2 ml salt
and milled black pepper, and sprinkle over
the dough before baking.
Olive oil glaze: brush the rolls/bread with
olive oil instead of glaze, and sprinkle
with garlic and herb seasoning and milled
black pepper.

SAVOURY BREAD STICKS

Makes 16–24 bread sticks, depending on size

*Great for snacking or to serve with soup,
salads or an outdoor meal.*

White Bread dough (page 86)
SAVOURY COATING
100 ml finely grated parmesan or
    pecorino cheese
5 ml mixed dried herbs
2 ml garlic and herb seasoning
1 ml cayenne pepper
1 ml paprika
2 ml coarse salt (optional)

1 Grease two medium baking trays.
2 Prepare the dough, following steps 1–3.
  Punch down and roll out onto a floured
  surface into a rectangle of about
  25 x 15 x 2 cm. Cut into strips about
  20 mm wide.
3 Combine the ingredients for the coating.
  Roll each strip in the savoury coating,
  and place onto the tray, twisting them
  slightly lengthwise.
4 Set aside to rise for 15 minutes. Meanwhile,
  preheat the oven to 180°C. Bake for
  8–10 minutes until golden and crisp. Allow
  to cool on a wire rack.

COOK'S NOTES
• Bread sticks last for a week or more
in airtight containers.
• If preferred, omit the coating, brush with
egg and water, and sprinkle with poppy and
sesame seeds or coarse salt.

SEMOLINA AND CHEDDAR ROLLS

Makes about 24 rolls

The addition of semolina creates a lovely texture, a nutty flavour and a crispy crust.

120 g (250 ml) Golden Cloud cake flour
10 g sachet instant yeast
200 ml milk
100 ml hot water
5 ml salt
50 g (50 ml) butter or hard margarine,
    cut into cubes and softened
1 egg
250 g (375 ml) Golden Cloud semolina
180 g (375 ml) extra Golden Cloud cake
    flour (approximate amount)
100 g (250 ml) grated cheddar cheese
milk for brushing
garlic and herb seasoning

1 Grease a large baking tray. Mix together the first measure of flour and yeast in a mixing bowl, or the bowl of an electric mixer fitted with the dough hook.
2 Add the milk, water, salt, butter or margarine, egg, and semolina to the flour and yeast mixture. Mix well. Add sufficient of the extra flour to form a soft dough, and knead for about 5 minutes (with the electric mixer), or turn out the dough onto a floured surface and knead by hand for 6–8 minutes, until smooth and elastic. Return the dough to the bowl, cover, and set aside to rise for about 40 minutes, until doubled in bulk.
3 Turn the dough out onto a floured surface. Flatten slightly, and sprinkle with the cheese. Knead until the cheese has just been incorporated. Pinch off egg-sized pieces, form into balls, and place slightly apart onto the tray. Set aside to rise, uncovered, in a protected spot for about 20 minutes, until doubled in bulk. Preheat the oven to 200°C.
4 Brush the rolls with milk, and sprinkle with seasoning. Bake for about 20 minutes, until firm and golden. Cool on a wire rack.

CARAMEL CREAM BUNS

Makes about 24 buns

Serve as a dessert with coffee.

Rich White Bread dough (page 86)
500 ml fresh or long-life cream
80 g (100 ml) brown sugar

1 Grease two medium rectangular ovenproof glass dishes. Prepare the dough, following steps 1–3.
2 Punch down lightly, and pinch off golf ball-sized pieces. Shape neatly and place into the dishes, about 10 mm apart.
3 Mix together the cream and brown sugar. Spoon half the mixture onto the buns, and set aside until doubled in bulk. Meanwhile preheat the oven to 180°C.
4 Spoon the remaining cream mixture onto the rolls, and bake for about 20 minutes, until well risen, cooked through and nicely browned. Allow to cool for a while. Serve from the dish.

COOK'S NOTES
• For spicy, nutty flavoured cream buns, add chopped nuts and ground cinnamon to the caramel glaze.
• For savoury buns, omit the brown sugar and add 10 ml garlic and herb seasoning, approximately 10 ml crushed fresh garlic and 15 ml chopped fresh parsley to the cream.

CHEESE BUNS

Makes about 24 buns, depending on size

Serve these delicious rolls while they are still warm, as a snack or with soup or salad.

Rich White Bread dough (page 86)
300 g (750 ml) grated cheddar cheese
    (approximate amount)
Red Sprinkle Mix (page 12)

1 Grease two 26–28 cm cake tins, or one large baking tray.
2 Prepare the dough, following steps 1–3. Divide in half, and roll each half out to a thickness of 20 mm. Sprinkle with the cheese and roll up like a swiss roll. Cut the rolls into neat slices about 25 mm thick and arrange, cut side down and close together, into the tins or onto the tray. Sprinkle with Red Sprinkle Mix, and set aside until doubled in bulk. Meanwhile preheat the oven to 180°C.
3 Bake for about 25 minutes until golden, and a cake-tester comes out clean. Allow to cool for a few minutes in the tins or tray.
4 Loosen the buns and turn out carefully onto a wire rack. Just before serving, break apart.

COOK'S NOTES
• For more flavourful cheese buns, add chopped, cooked bacon or mushrooms, and/or other pizza-style ingredients to the filling, and top with chopped fresh parsley and garlic.
• If preferred, make buns out of half the dough (use only half the cheese), and make a small loaf out of the remaining dough.
• For cheese and onion rolls, knead about 125 ml fried, chopped onion into the dough with the cheese, and bake in a 26 cm loaf tin.

BREAD ROLLS

Rolls can be made from almost any bread dough, as long as it's firm enough to knead. Bear in mind that rolls double in size during the baking process.

SHAPING BREAD ROLLS

DINNER ROLLS
Punch down risen bread dough. Pinch off golf ball-sized portions, shape neatly and pack, slightly apart if you want them to connect while baking, or well apart if you don't, onto well-greased baking trays, or into round cake tins. For a special effect, score the tops once or twice or crosswise with a sharp knife.

HAMBURGER BUNS
Prepare white or brown bread dough, and cut out large round rolls.

ELONGATED ROLLS
Roll out risen dough onto a well-floured surface, to a thickness of about 20 mm. Cut with a finger-shaped or rectangular cutter, such as an empty, cleaned anchovy tin. Or pinch off balls of dough and roll into finger shapes. Shape neatly, and place onto well-greased baking trays, slightly apart. If you wish, score deeply lengthwise, and dust generously with flour.

RING-SHAPED ROLLS
Roll out the dough and cut with a doughnut cutter, or with a large round cutter, using a smaller cutter to remove the centre.

PLAITED ROLLS
See instructions for the plaiting as given in the recipe for Kitke (page 94).

CLOVER LEAF ROLLS
Punch down risen dough and pinch off tiny balls, just larger than marbles. Grease the cups of muffin tins, and pack three balls into each cup. Use three different kinds of dough if you wish, flavour the individual balls – one with grated cheese, one with mixed dried herbs and one with crushed garlic and milled black pepper.

FINISHING BREAD ROLLS

Rolls may be left plain, but a glaze or topping adds a professional touch. Toppings are included with specific recipes, but these are the most popular.

GLAZE
Beat together 1 egg and 15 ml milk or water, and brush onto the rolls before rising and baking. For larger loaves, dilute the glaze with a little extra water or milk to prevent the crust from browning too much during the baking process.

GLAZE AND SEED
After glazing, sprinkle with poppy, sesame or sunflower seeds.

FLOUR COATING
For soft, floury rolls, coat or sprinkle with flour after shaping. Use cake or wholewheat flour, depending on the dough.

SALT WATER GLAZE
For a crisp, salty crust, stir 5 ml salt into 60 ml water, and brush onto the rolls after shaping, and again just before baking. To make the rolls even crisper, brush again halfway through baking. Coarse salt can also be sprinkled over.

BAKING BREAD ROLLS

After shaping, pack rolls onto baking trays and finish as preferred. Set aside to rise in a warm, protected spot, until doubled in bulk. Preheat the oven to 180°C. Bake for 15–25 minutes, depending on size, until the rolls are well risen, firm and light golden; don't allow them to become too brown or too dry. Allow to cool on a wire rack. Serve warm or cool.

STORING, FREEZING AND REHEATING BREAD ROLLS
Store in airtight containers after the rolls have cooled completely. To freshen, reheat for a few minutes in an oven preheated to 160°C. If not used within a day, freeze them. Large rolls should be thawed for a short while, but smaller rolls can be reheated from frozen. For a crisp, just-baked effect, reheat the rolls in oven bags, which will prevent them from drying out.

TO BAKE ROLLS FOR FREEZING
Half-bake the rolls until well risen and firm, and very lightly coloured. Allow to cool on a wire rack, and freeze in airtight containers. Just before serving, place on a baking tray and bake at 180°C for about 10 minutes until crisp and golden.

SWEET PIES & PASTRIES

Making pastry is extraordinarily satisfying, and, with the recipes that follow, as easy as pie! And, presenting to loved ones a freshly baked tart, warm from the oven and dusted with icing sugar, is one of life's special pleasures.

Pastry chefs of days gone by were renowned for baking complex creations, which took time, effort and considerable skill. Happily, modern-day pies are far more casual and homely, more natural in appearance and more wholesome in content.

They can also be rustled up quick-as-a-lick, with the assistance of handy helpers – a food processor or electric mixer. Use the metal blade in your processor, or the dough hook in your mixer. Techniques and watchpoints, however, are extremely important, and using chilled ingredients, working quickly and handling the dough with a light hand will ensure crisp, feather-light home bakes that melt in the mouth.

Fillings are as diverse as custard, fruit (fresh or tinned) and nuts – all nutritious and tasty.

A slice of tart should be beautifully presented: serving with a complementary sauce, tasty topping, or fresh garnish such as flowers, leaves or roasted nuts requires no effort, and makes the plainest pie perfect, and your guests feel pampered.

Enjoy exploring these sweet pies and pastries, which include the best of many old favourites, as well as some 'new' classics, and lots of ideas for home industries and catering.

Spicy Apple Pie with Almond Topping page 103

Greek Custard Slices page 101

Pecan Cream Cheese Pie page 108

APPLE TARTLETS

Makes 12 tartlets

FEATHER-LIGHT SWEET PASTRY
120 g (250 ml) Golden Cloud cake flour
60 ml cornflour
2 ml baking powder
30 ml castor sugar
100 g (100) butter or hard margarine
1 egg
2 ml vanilla essence
pinch salt

APPLE FILLING
400 g jar apple sauce
50 ml sugar
50 ml cornflour
5–10 ml lemon juice (optional)
765 g tin unsweetened pie apples
icing sugar and cinnamon for dusting

1 Place all the ingredients for the pastry into a food processor, or electric mixer fitted with the dough hook. Blend or mix until the dough just holds together. Knead very lightly, until smooth. Roll into a ball, wrap in clingfilm and refrigerate for at least 30 minutes, or for up to a day.
2 Generously grease 12 cups of a standard muffin tin. Roll out the pastry thinly (about 4 mm thick) onto a lightly floured surface. Cut out 10 cm circles, and press neatly into the muffin cups. Set aside remaining pastry. Refrigerate until well chilled.
3 To make the filling: place the apple sauce, sugar, cornflour and lemon juice (if using) into a saucepan. Bring to the boil, stirring constantly, and simmer for 2 minutes. Cut the apples coarsely, and mix into the sauce. Allow to cool to room temperature.

4 Meanwhile, preheat the oven to 180°C.
5 Spoon the filling into the lined muffin cups, coarsely grate the remaining pastry, and sprinkle evenly onto the tartlets.
6 Bake for about 30 minutes, until the pastry is golden and firm. Allow the tarts to cool in the muffin cups for at least 15 minutes, then remove carefully with a small palette knife. Dust with icing sugar and cinnamon.

APPLE TARTLETS VARIATION

Fresh Apple Tartlets
Replace the apple sauce with fresh apples. Place 4–5 peeled, sliced apples into a saucepan with a little water. Cover and simmer until tender; mash. Or place into a bowl (without liquid) and microwave, uncovered, on High for 6–8 minutes.

GOLDEN CLOUD HOME BAKES
100

GREEK CUSTARD SLICES

Makes 16 slices or squares

SEMOLINA CUSTARD
1.25 litres milk
200 g (250 ml) Golden Cloud semolina
6 eggs
50 g (50 ml) butter or hard margarine
150 g (200 ml) sugar
pinch salt
5 ml vanilla essence
5 ml finely grated lemon zest (optional)

PHYLLO PASTRY
12 sheets ready-made phyllo pastry
100 g (100 ml) butter or hard
   margarine, melted

LEMON SYRUP
200 g (250 ml) sugar
325 ml water
30 ml lemon juice
1 cinnamon stick

1 Preheat the oven to 170°C. Set out a deep, rectangular ovenproof dish (30 x 20 cm).

2 To make the custard, heat the milk to boiling point. Stir in the semolina. Bring to the boil, stirring with a whisk, until smooth and thickened. Simmer for 5 minutes.

3 Beat the eggs in a jug. Stir in a little of the hot mixture. Pour the egg and milk mixture back into the saucepan, and mix well. Beat in the butter or margarine, sugar, salt, vanilla essence and lemon zest (if using).

4 Brush the dish with melted butter or margarine, and line with half the pastry, brushing each sheet with melted butter.

5 Pour the filling into the dish. Cover the custard with the remaining sheets of pastry, brushing each sheet with melted butter. Neaten the edges, and brush the top with the remaining butter or margarine. Bake for about 35 minutes, until golden and set. Allow to cool.

6 Meanwhile, place the ingredients for the syrup into a saucepan. Bring to the boil, stirring constantly. Simmer gently for 10 minutes. Cool to lukewarm, then pour over the baked tart.

7 Allow to cool, then chill in the fridge until the tart is firm. It can be kept in the fridge for up to 4 days. To serve, cut into neat slices or squares.

COOK'S NOTE
Omit the syrup, cool the pie and dust with cinnamon-flavoured icing sugar (50 ml icing sugar and 5 ml cinnamon), and you'll have bougasta.

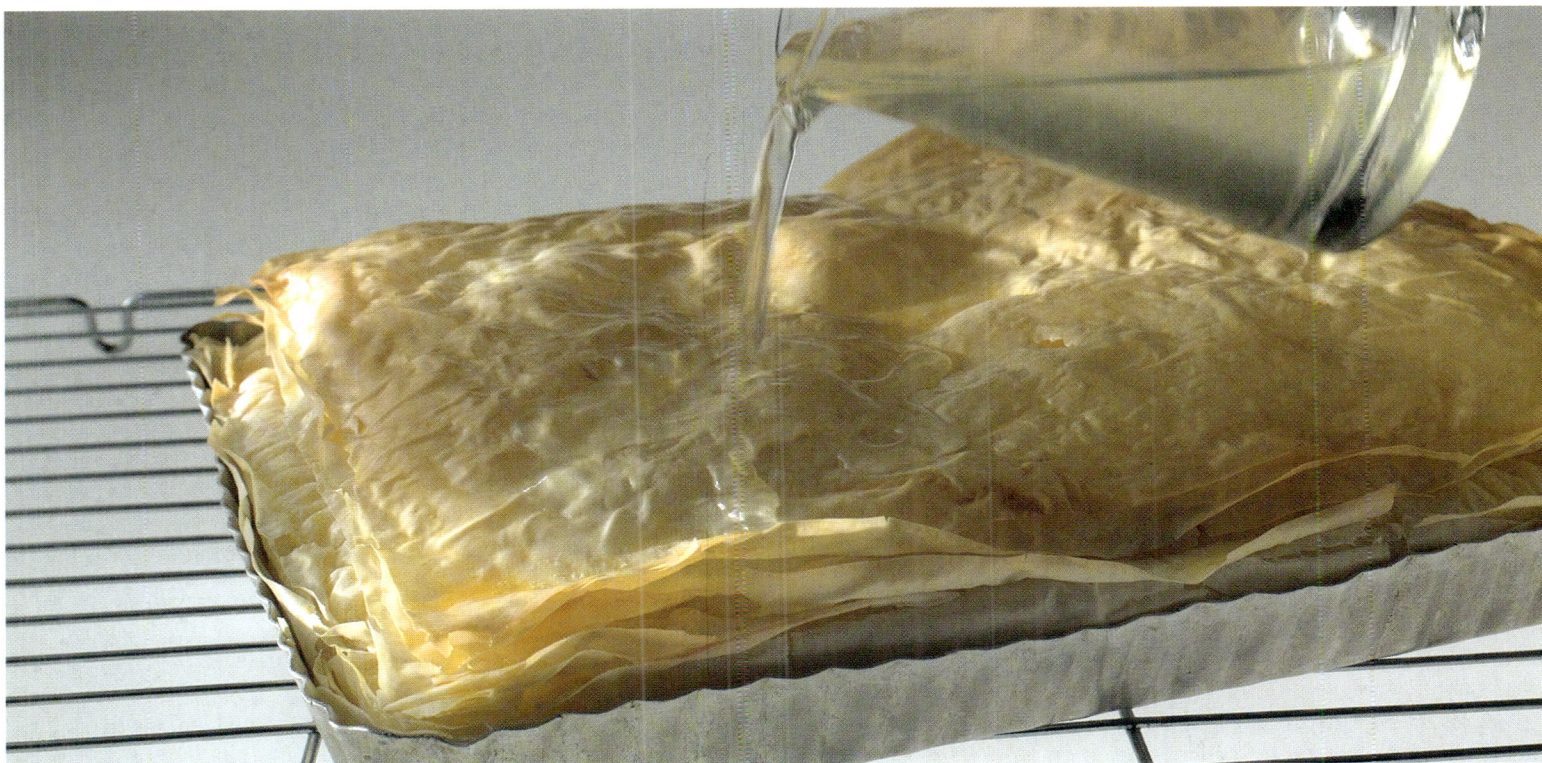

CHOUX PASTRY CUSTARD SLICES

Makes 12 slices

These are similar to Polish karpatka. They are best after they have been cooled and refrigerated for a few hours.

CUSTARD FILLING
60 g (60 ml) butter or hard margarine
100 g (200 ml) Golden Cloud cake flour
1 litre milk
1 ml salt
5 ml vanilla essence
2 ml almond essence
10 ml brandy (optional)
3 eggs, separated
100 g (125 ml) sugar
SOFT CHOUX PASTRY
350 ml water
100 g (100 ml) butter or hard margarine
pinch salt
120 g (250 ml) Golden Cloud cake flour
3–4 eggs
GARNISH
icing sugar for dusting

1 To make the custard, melt together the butter and flour in a heavy-based saucepan, stirring until crumbly. Remove from the heat. Beat in the milk. Bring to the boil, beating constantly, until the sauce becomes thick.

2 Add the salt, vanilla and almond essences and brandy (if using). Beat in the egg yolks and sugar. Cook over moderate heat, stirring constantly, until thick and bubbly.

3 Beat the egg whites to soft peaks and fold into the custard, until well combined. Allow to cool while making the pastry. Meanwhile preheat the oven to 180°C. Grease a deep rectangular dish (30 x 20 cm).

4 To make the choux pastry, place the water, butter or margarine and salt into a saucepan and bring to the boil. Add the flour and beat well, until a ball is formed. Transfer the dough to a bowl or the bowl of an electric mixer, and allow to cool for 5 minutes.

Beat in the eggs one at a time, beating well after each addition.

5 Spread about one-third of the of the pastry onto the base and up the sides of the dish. Spoon the remaining pastry into a piping bag fitted with a small star nozzle.

6 Spoon the custard into the dish, and smooth the top. Pipe pastry around the edge, then pipe the rest onto the custard in a trellis pattern. Bake for about 30 minutes, until the top is golden brown and firm.

7 Switch off the oven and allow the pie to cool in the oven for 10 minutes. Place on a wire rack and allow to cool to room temperature, then refrigerate for at least 2 hours before cutting into slices. Dust with icing sugar.

CHOUX PASTRY VARIATION

Chocolate Eclairs or Chocolate Puffs
Prepare the pastry, using only 250 ml water. Pipe or blob choux pastry onto a wet baking tray and bake at 200°C for 10 minutes, then reduce the temperature to 160°C and bake for 15–30 minutes more until the pastry is no longer 'sweaty'. Allow to cool on a wire rack, fill with whipped cream, and coat with your favourite chocolate glaze. Recipes are on page 80.

SPICY APPLE PIE WITH ALMOND TOPPING

Makes 1 large pie

Feather-light Sweet Pastry (page 100)

APPLE FILLING
765 g tin pie apples, coarsely chopped
20–40 g (50–100 ml) coarsely chopped
    pecan nuts
50 ml lemon juice
50 ml smooth apricot jam
30 ml brown sugar
50 g (50 ml) butter or hard margarine,
    melted
5 ml cornflour or custard powder
5 ml ground cinnamon
pinch ground cloves

ALMOND TOPPING
50 g (50 ml) butter or hard margarine
50 g (125 ml) ground almonds
60 g (100 ml) Golden Cloud cake flour
50 ml castor sugar
2 eggs
1 drop almond essence
icing sugar for dusting

1 Preheat the oven to 180 °C. Generously
  grease a deep 25 cm pie dish.
2 Prepare the pastry as described for Apple
  Tartlets (page 100), but don't chill or roll it
  out. Simply turn it into the pie dish, and
  press evenly onto the base and up the sides,
  thinning the pastry in the corners.
3 To make the apple filling, place the apples
  and nuts into a mixing bowl. In a separate,
  small bowl, mix together all the remaining
  filling ingredients. Add to the apples and
  toss to combine. Spoon into the prepared
  pastry. Smooth the top.
4 Almond topping: place the topping
  ingredients into the bowl of a food processor
  or electric mixer, and process or mix to a
  smooth, thick batter. Place spoonfuls of the
  batter onto the apple filling and spread
  evenly to cover.
5 Bake for about 30 minutes, until the topping
  is light golden brown. Remove from the oven

and allow the pie to cool completely – for at
least 1 hour – to allow the filling to set. The
pie tends to break if served hot from the
oven. (After the initial cooling the pie may be
reheated and will slice neatly.) Dust lightly
with icing sugar and serve.

COOK'S NOTES
• Substitute marmalade or any other jam for
  the apricot jam, and omit the nuts in the
  filling for a more economical pie.
• Substitute biscuit crumbs for the ground
  almonds in the topping.

BUTTERMILK PIE

Makes 1 large pie

*An easy crustless pie – delicious as is or
topped with whipped cream or fruit sauce.*

3 eggs
75 g (75 ml) butter or hard margarine,
  cut into cubes and softened
150 g (200 ml) sugar
500 ml buttermilk
5 ml vanilla essence
120 g (250 ml) Golden Cloud cake flour
5 ml baking powder
pinch salt
500 ml milk

1 Preheat the oven to 180°C. Grease a deep
  rectangular ovenproof dish (30 x 20 cm),
  or a deep 25 cm pie dish.
2 Separate the eggs and place yolks and whites
  into separate bowls. Beat the whites until
  stiff peaks form, and set aside. Add the
  butter or margarine and sugar to the yolks,
  and beat well, until pale and light.
3 Add the buttermilk, vanilla essence, flour,
  baking powder and salt to the yolk mixture,
  and beat well, until smooth. Gradually add
  the milk, beating to a thin batter. Pour the
  batter onto the egg white and fold in gently,
  until evenly combined.
4 Pour the filling into the prepared dish, and
  bake for about 40 minutes, until light golden
  brown and set. Allow to cool. The pie keeps
  well in the fridge for up to 4 days. Cut into
  neat squares or wedges to serve.

BUTTERMILK PIE VARIATIONS

Lemon Buttermilk Pie
Add 15–30 ml freshly squeezed lemon juice,
and increase the sugar to 200 g (250 ml).
Yoghurt Pie
Use natural yoghurt instead of buttermilk.
Crustless Milk Tart
Use milk instead of buttermilk, and sprinkle
the pie with ground cinnamon before baking.

LEMON MERINGUE PIE

Makes 1 large pie

CRISP CRUMB CRUST
200 g crisp biscuits (see Cook's notes)
50 g (50 ml) butter or hard margarine
LEMON FILLING
3 x 397 g tins full-cream sweetened
  condensed milk
175 ml hot water
200 ml freshly squeezed lemon juice
6 egg yolks
2 ml cornflour
MERINGUE TOPPING
6 egg whites
1 ml cream of tartar
15 ml cornflour
150 g (200 ml) sugar
2 ml vanilla essence

1 Place the oven rack at one level below the
  centre in the oven. Preheat the oven to
  170°C. Grease a 28 cm pie dish.
2 Place the crust ingredients into a food
  processor, and process until evenly blended.
  Turn into the pie dish and press firmly and
  evenly onto the base and up the sides.
3 To make the filling, place the condensed milk,
  water and lemon juice into a bowl and beat
  until well combined. Beat in the egg yolks.
  Pour the mixture into the prepared crust –
  do this over the back of a large spoon to
  prevent the crust from breaking.
4 Dust the filling very lightly with cornflour,
  using a fine tea strainer, to allow the
  meringue to stick to the filling.
5 Beat the egg whites and cream of tartar until
  stiff. Sprinkle in the cornflour and continue
  beating, adding the sugar gradually, until
  stiff and glossy. Beat in the vanilla essence.
6 Spoon and swirl (or pipe) the meringue onto
  the filling, covering the edges of the crust to
  prevent the meringue from shrinking away
  from the sides.
7 Bake for 25–30 minutes, until the filling
  is set and the meringue is golden. Reduce
  the temperature slightly or cover loosely
  with foil if the meringue darkens too quickly
  or too much.
8 Reduce the oven temperature to 160°C, open
  the door slightly and leave the pie in the
  oven for 10 minutes. Switch off the oven,
  and leave the pie in the oven to cool
  completely for crisp, dry meringue.
9 Refrigerate the cooled pie, uncovered, for
  at least 1 hour before serving. Cover only
  when cold and dry, to prevent the meringue
  from seeping.

COOK'S NOTES
• Use any variety of biscuits you like,
for example shortbread biscuits, or half
shortbread, half wholemeal digestive biscuits.
• For smaller pies, bake in two 20–22 cm
pie dishes, or halve the recipe and make
one small pie.
• Refrigerate in a covered (not airtight)
container, for up to 5 days. Or, freeze
in an airtight container. Remove the pie
about 1 hour before serving and thaw,
uncovered, at room temperature.
• Replace 100 ml of the lemon juice with
100 ml fresh or tinned crushed pineapple,
or fresh or tinned granadilla
pulp (110 g tin).

BAKED CHEESECAKE

Makes 1 large cheesecake

CINNAMON SHORTBREAD CRUST

200 g packet shortbread biscuits

50 g (50 ml) butter or
hard margarine

7 ml ground cinnamon

CHEESE FILLING

6 eggs

750 g creamed cottage cheese
(at room temperature)

10 ml vanilla essence

50 g (100 ml) Golden Cloud cake flour

150 g (200 ml) sugar

30 ml lemon juice

250 ml cream

125 ml sour cream or
extra cream

1 Preheat the oven to 150°C. Line the base of a 28–30 cm springform tin with baking paper. Grease the paper as well as the tin.

2 Place the crust ingredients into a food processor, and process until evenly blended. Press onto the base of the tin.

3 Separate the eggs and place the whites and yolks into separate bowls. Add the remaining filling ingredients to the yolks, and beat very well for about 5 minutes. Beat the egg whites until firm and glossy. Add the egg white to the yolk mixture, and fold in gently but thoroughly.

4 Pour the filling into the prepared tin and bake for about $1\frac{1}{4}$ hours, until well risen, light golden brown, and completely set if lightly pressed in the centre.

5 Partially open the oven door and allow the cake to cool for at least 1 hour. Allow to cool completely on a wire rack before removing the rim of the tin.

6 Remove the cake – with the paper lining – from the base of the tin, and place onto the base of an airtight container. Keep the cake covered and refrigerated until required. When quite cold and firm, slip a large spatula or two egglifters between the paper and the crust and transfer carefully to a serving platter.

7 Serve plain or garnish with cinnamon sugar or whipped cream. Serve Fresh Fruit Sauce (page 83) separately, if desired.

COOK'S NOTES

• Replace the biscuit crust with Feather-light Sweet Pastry (page 100).

• This cake can be refrigerated for up to 5 days.

CREAM CHEESE AND FRUIT FANTASY

Makes 8–10 servings

A festive summertime no-bake dessert or cake beyond description!

CINNAMON CRUMB CRUST
125 g packet finger biscuits
1 ml ground cinnamon
60 g (60 ml) butter or hard margarine
15 ml sherry or citrus-based liqueur (optional)

FRUITY CREAM CHEESE FILLING
15 ml gelatine
200 ml unsweetened fruit juice (apricot, peach, orange or mango)
250 g (250 ml) creamed cottage cheese
250 ml cream
60 g (125 ml) icing sugar
5 ml vanilla essence

FRUIT AND CREAM TOPPING
25 g strawberries, washed, hulled and sliced (approximate amount)
2–3 kiwi fruit, peeled and sliced
1 banana, peeled and sliced
12 black grapes halved and seeded, or 125 ml fresh or drained tinned blueberries (approximate amount)
250 ml cream
30 ml icing sugar

1 Generously grease a 25 cm pie dish, or line the base of a 22 cm springform tin with waxed paper or baking paper. Grease the paper as well as the sides of the tin.
2 Place the crust ingredients into a food processor and process until evenly blended. Press the mixture onto the base of the dish or tin.
3 To make the filling, place the gelatine into a bowl or jug with at least a 500 ml capacity, and pour in the fruit juice. Place over simmering water, or microwave on Medium for about 2 minutes, until the gelatine has dissolved. Allow to cool for 5 minutes. Beat in about 50 ml of the cream cheese.

4 Place the remaining cream cheese into a bowl, and add the gelatine mixture. Beat with an electric beater until smooth. Beat the cream with the icing sugar until stiff. Add to the cream cheese mixture, together with the vanilla essence, and gently fold together, until evenly combined. Pour into the prepared dish or tin, and refrigerate for at least 3 hours, until set. Remove the tart from the springform tin.
5 Prepare the fruit for the topping. Banana (or other fruit that tends to discolour) should be brushed with lemon juice mixed with a little water. Beat together the cream and icing sugar until stiff. Spoon into a piping bag fitted with a rosette nozzle. Pipe cream rosettes around the edge of the pie and from the centre, leaving spaces in between to fill with the fruit.
6 Arrange fruit between and on top of the cream, and refrigerate until required – preferably no more than 1 hour. Cut into wedges and serve.

> ## COOK'S NOTES
> - This pie can be covered and refrigerated – without the topping – for up to 3 days before completing and serving.
> - Use shortbread, digestive and/or ginger biscuits instead of finger biscuits.
> - Use any fruit you wish, according to preference and availability. Although fresh fruit is better, drained tinned fruit can be used.

PECAN CREAM CHEESE PIE

Makes 1 medium pie

QUICK SWEET PASTRY
120 g (250 ml) Golden Cloud cake flour
50 ml sugar
60 g (70 ml) butter or hard margarine
1 egg yolk
pinch salt
30 ml milk (approximate amount)
CREAM CHEESE FILLING
500 g creamed cottage cheese
50 ml sugar
10 ml vanilla essence
1 egg
PECAN TOPPING
200 ml golden or maple syrup (warmed)
3 eggs
5 ml vanilla essence
200 g (500 ml) whole pecan nuts

1 Preheat the oven to 180°C. Grease a 22 cm pie dish.
2 Place all the ingredients for the pastry into a food processor; process until just smooth. Press the pastry evenly into the dish, and neaten the edges.
3 Cover completely with light foil, pressing it onto the pastry so that it retains its shape while baking. Bake for 10 minutes; remove from the oven.
4 To make the filling, place all the ingredients into a mixing bowl, or the bowl of a food processor, and mix or blend well. Pour into the pastry shell.
5 Reserve about one-third of the nuts; coarsely chop the rest. Sprinkle the chopped nuts onto the filling.
6 Beat together the syrup, eggs and vanilla essence, and spoon over the nuts and filling. Decorate the edge with reserved nuts. Place into the oven, reduce the temperature to 160°C, and bake for about 40 minutes, until the filling is just set, but is still a little soft in the centre. Allow to cool. Refrigerate for up to three days, but serve at room temperature, as is or with whipped cream.

MILK TART

Makes 1 large tart

RICH SWEET PASTRY

120 g (250 ml) Golden Cloud cake flour
pinch salt
2 ml baking powder
30 ml sugar
75 g (75 ml) butter or hard margarine,
    softened
1 egg
few drops of water, if necessary

MILK FILLING

1 litre milk
1 cinnamon stick
90 g (175 ml) Golden Cloud cake flour
pinch salt
60 g (60 ml) butter or hard margarine
100 g (125 ml) sugar
5 ml vanilla essence
1 ml almond essence (optional)
4 eggs
5 ml baking powder
ground cinnamon for sprinkling

1 Preheat the oven to 200°C. Generously grease a deep 26 cm pie plate, or a shallow 28 cm pie plate, or two 20 cm pie plates.
2 Place the ingredients for the crust into a bowl, and mix by hand to a smooth, soft dough. Press the dough into the pie plate/s very thinly – it should almost be transparent. Refrigerate while making the filling.
3 To make the filling, heat 750 ml of the milk with the cinnamon stick to boiling point. Mix the remainder of the milk with the flour to a smooth paste. Mix a little of the hot milk into the paste; pour back into the saucepan.
4 Bring to the boil, stirring with a whisk until smooth and thick. Simmer gently for 2 minutes. Remove from the heat, and beat in the salt, butter or margarine, sugar and vanilla and almond (if using) essences.
5 Separate the eggs into separate bowls. Beat a little of the hot sauce into the yolks, then pour it back into the saucepan, and mix well. Allow to cool. Beat in the baking powder.
6 Beat the egg whites until soft peaks form. Add to the cooled sauce, and mix in gently, until evenly blended. Pour the filling into the pie plate/s, making it/them almost full. Sprinkle lightly with cinnamon.
7 Place the tart/s into the oven, reduce heat to 180°C, and bake for about 12 minutes (small tarts) or 15–18 minutes (larger tart), until risen and golden, but not completely set.
8 Switch off the oven, partially open the door and leave the tart/s in the oven for about 10 minutes more to cool and set gradually.

COOK'S NOTES

For a more elegant serving, prepare a cinnamon syrup: place 125 ml water, 125 ml sugar, 5 ml cinnamon and a drop of vanilla essence into a small saucepan. Bring to the boil, stirring constantly, and simmer for 5 minutes. Allow to cool. Pour a little syrup onto plates, place slices of milk tart on top, and decorate with whipped cream and roasted flaked almonds (see page 12).

SAVOURY
SNACKS & PIES

Savouries make great snacks, starters, and light meals, and are especially good with pre-meal drinks if you're entertaining. And there's lots to choose from if you're planning a casual snack or meal in front of the television.

All are tried and tested, and perfect for home and home-industry use. Several savoury biscuit recipes are included as an alternative to the more commonly baked sweet biscuits. These are quick and easy to make, and great to serve for between-meal snacks, or with cheese after a meal. And children love to take savoury biscuits instead of sandwiches to school.

Since the first pizzeria opened in Naples almost 200 years ago, pizza has taken the world by storm. The recipe on page 124 will become a firm family favourite. Pizzas range fairly dramatically

in size, so it's difficult to accurately determine the amount of topping required, so have a generous amount ready. Pizzas are best served fresh from the oven. Refrigerate the dough to retard the rising process, or refrigerate the completed pizzas, loosely covered for up to 2 hours before baking.

Like all the recipes in Home Bakes, a host of variations is offered to appeal to the widest range of tastes and pockets, and to broaden the baker's scope and make room for experimentation.

For those cooks who enjoy working with pastry, there are many variations of savoury pastries in this chapter; feel free to swap them around if you wish. Most of the recipes make one large pie, sufficient for 12 small slices, or 6–8 servings for a light meal. Round the menu off with a salad.

Mediterranean Phyllo Pie page 119

Feta Pie page 122

Potato, Leek and Cheese Pie page 120

Chicken and Broccoli Pie page 121

CHEESY CORNFLAKE CRACKLES

Makes about 36 biscuits

Quick to make, and much more delicious than store-bought cheese biscuits, these are favourites for party tables and lunchboxes.

1 egg
50 ml milk
100 g (100 ml) butter or hard
   margarine, cut into cubes and
   softened
100 g (250 ml) grated cheddar cheese
2 ml salt
pinch cayenne pepper
140 g (250 ml) Golden Cloud
   self-raising flour
60 g (250 ml) crushed cornflakes
seasoning spice (see Cook's notes)

1 Preheat the oven to 180°C. Grease one large or two medium baking trays.
2 Beat together the egg and milk; reserve 15 ml for the glaze. Place the butter or margarine, cheese, salt, cayenne pepper, flour and cornflakes into a mixing bowl, and mix together. Add the egg and milk mixture, and knead by hand to a moderately firm, irregular dough.
3 Roll heaped teaspoonfuls of the dough into neat balls. Place 50 mm apart onto the baking tray/s and flatten with a fork. Brush with the reserved glaze, and sprinkle with a seasoning of your choice.
4 Bake for 12–15 minutes, until the biscuits are pale golden and firm. Switch off the oven, open the door slightly, and leave the biscuits in the oven for 15 minutes more to become crisp. Cool on a wire rack.

> ## COOK'S NOTE
> Tasty seasoning includes paprika, garlic and herb, or barbecue seasoning, Red Sprinkle Mix (page 12), cayenne pepper, and Mexican or Cajun spices.

PARMESAN AND ROSEMARY BISCUITS

Makes about 50 biscuits

120 g (250 ml) Golden Cloud cake flour
30 ml Golden Cloud self-raising flour
1 ml salt
5 ml sugar
10 ml dried rosemary
pinch cayenne pepper
125 g (150 ml) butter or hard
   margarine, cut into cubes and
   softened
30 ml grated parmesan cheese
15 ml lemon juice

1 Place all the ingredients into the bowl of a food processor, or electric mixer, and process or mix to a dough. Don't overmix.
2 Turn the dough out onto a floured surface, and shape into a roll about 25 mm in diameter. Wrap in clingfilm and refrigerate for at least 2 hours, or up to several days.
3 Preheat the oven to 190°C. Grease a medium baking tray. Slice the dough roll thinly into biscuits about 6 mm thick. Place on baking trays and bake for about 12 minutes, until golden and crisp. Cool on a wire rack.

SAVOURY BISCOTTI

Makes about 40 biscotti, depending on size

Perfect with pâté, cheese and salad.

100 g (100 ml) butter or hard
   margarine, cut into cubes and
   softened
300 g (600 ml) Golden Cloud cake flour
7 ml baking powder
7 ml salt
1 ml milled black pepper
60 ml chopped fresh parsley
60 ml chopped capers
50 ml olive oil
100 ml milk
2 eggs

1 Place all the ingredients into a mixing bowl, or the bowl of a food processor, and mix or process just until the dough holds together. Press into a ball and chill for at least 1 hour, but preferably overnight.
2 Preheat the oven to 180°C. Grease a medium baking tray. Divide the dough in half and roll each half into a sausage about 30 cm long. Place the rolls on the baking tray, allowing at least 60 mm in between for spreading.
3 Slice diagonally into thin slices about 10 mm wide, but keep the rolls intact while baking. This simplifies slicing, and reduces crumbling when slicing after baking.
4 Bake for about 30 minutes, until the biscuits are golden and firm. Remove from the oven and allow to cool for a few minutes. Reduce the temperature to 100°C.
5 Cut the biscuits through with a sharp knife. Lay the slices flat on the baking tray, and return to the oven. Leave the oven door slightly ajar to allow moisture to escape, and allow the biscuits to dry out for 30–45 minutes until crisp. Allow to cool.

> ## COOK'S NOTE
> Replace the capers with fresh basil or rosemary to vary the flavour.

PECAN-PAPRIKA BISCUITS

Makes about 40 biscuits

*Serve as pre-dinner snacks with cocktails,
or as part of a cheese board.*

2 eggs
30 ml water
120 g (250 ml) Golden Cloud cake flour
70 g (125 ml) Golden Cloud
    self-raising flour
2 ml salt
5 ml paprika
125 g (150 ml) butter or hard
    margarine, cut into cubes and
    softened
50 g pecan nuts, finely chopped and
    roasted (see page 12)
Red Sprinkle Mix (page 12), or cayenne
    pepper, or garlic and herb seasoning

1 Beat together the eggs and water. Set aside.
2 Place the flours, salt, paprika and butter or
  margarine into a mixing bowl, or the bowl of
  a food processor, and process or rub
  together until crumbly. Mix in the nuts.
  Gradually add sufficient of the egg mixture
  until the dough holds together and forms a
  ball. Cover and refrigerate for at least
  30 minutes, or for several hours if possible.
3 Preheat the oven to 180°C. Grease two
  medium baking trays. Roll out the dough on
  a floured surface to a thickness of about
  6 mm. Cut into 40 mm squares or rounds,
  and place on the tray.
4 Brush with the remaining egg mixture, and
  sprinkle lightly with seasoning. Bake for
  about 20 minutes, until the biscuits are
  lightly browned. Allow to cool on the baking
  trays for 5 minutes. Transfer to a wire rack
  to cool completely.

> ## COOK'S NOTE
> The nuts can be replaced by 50 g (125 ml)
> coarsely grated hard cheese such as cheddar,
> parmesan or pecorino.

POPPY SEED AND ONION CRACKERS

Makes about 60 biscuits

*Thin, versatile crackers to serve as a nibble
with cheese or pâté.*

15 ml dried onion flakes
60 ml warm water
240 g (500 ml) Golden Cloud cake flour
5 ml baking powder
5 ml sugar
5 ml salt
1 ml white pepper
75 ml poppy seeds
2 eggs, lightly beaten
100 ml sunflower oil
a little extra cake flour

1 Preheat the oven to 180°C. Set out two large
  or three medium, ungreased baking trays.
2 Place the onion flakes into a bowl, pour over
  the water and set aside for at least 5 minutes.
3 Place the flour, baking powder, sugar, salt,
  pepper and poppy seeds into a mixing bowl,
  and stir to combine. Add the onion (and
  water), eggs and oil, and mix until the
  dough holds together. Gather into a ball,
  adding a little extra flour if necessary.
4 Roll out the dough thinly (2–3 mm) on a
  floured surface. Cut out with a 4 cm round
  cutter, and place on the baking trays, about
  30 mm apart. Gather the trimmings together
  and reroll until all the dough has been cut.
5 Bake for about 15 minutes, until the edges
  start to brown very lightly. Transfer to a wire
  rack to cool completely.

> ## COOK'S NOTES
> • The secret to the success of these biscuits lies in rolling out the dough very thinly and evenly.
> • Onion flakes can be replaced by 10 ml garlic and herb seasoning.

COCKTAIL SAUSAGE ROLLS

Makes 30–40 sausage rolls, depending on size

Home-made sausage rolls aren't nearly as much of a challenge as you may think. The secret is in the light, flaky soda water pastry, which can also be used for sweet or savoury pies.

SODA WATER PASTRY
250 g (280 ml) butter or hard
   margarine, ice cold
240 g (500 ml) Golden Cloud cake flour
2 ml cream of tartar
2 ml salt
30 ml brandy (optional)
175 ml chilled soda water (approximate
   amount)

SAUSAGE FILLING
500 g beef or pork sausages
500 g lean beef mince
2 eggs, lightly beaten
1 ml salt
1 ml worcestershire sauce (optional)
15 ml water

1 To make the pastry, grate the butter or margarine into a mixing bowl. Add the flour, cream of tartar and salt, and mix with a fork until the ingredients are evenly distributed.
2 Mix the brandy (if using) with 125 ml of the soda water, and add to the flour mixture. Mix with a fork, gradually adding more soda until the dough holds together in a medium-firm pastry; it will be irregular in colour and texture.
3 Lightly flour a worktop, and roll out the pastry with a floured rolling pin into an oblong about 20 mm thick. Fold into three layers, turn 90° and roll and fold again. Refrigerate for 20 minutes.
4 Repeat the rolling and folding twice more, until the pastry has been rolled and folded 6 times, and refrigerated twice. Refrigerate for at least 10 minutes more, or wrap in clingfilm and refrigerate overnight.

5 To make the filling, squeeze the sausage meat out of the casings into a bowl. Add the beef mince and mix. Measure 15 ml of the beaten egg into a cup and set aside for glazing. Mix the rest of the egg, salt and worcestershire sauce (if using) evenly into the sausage meat. Spoon into a piping bag fitted with a 2 cm nozzle.
6 Roll out the pastry into a 30 cm rectangle about 5 mm thick. Trim the left side straight. Pipe a strip of filling about 25 mm from the edge. Fold the pastry over the filling, extending it onto the pastry. Cut away the filled section and repeat the process until you have made several long rolls, and all the filling has been used.
7 Seal the edges of the pastry with a fork, and prick the top. Add the water to the egg, and brush onto the pastry. Mark the sausage rolls, making them approximately 50 mm in length, making deep indentations with the back of a knife; don't cut them through.
8 Grease two medium baking trays. Place the sausage rolls on the trays, allowing 30 mm in between the long rolls for rising and even browning. Refrigerate the rolls while preheating the oven to 190°C.
9 Place the trays into the oven and bake the sausage rolls for 15 minutes. Reduce the temperature to 170°C, and bake for another 10–15 minutes, until the pastry is crisp and golden brown, and the filling is cooked.
10 Allow the sausage rolls to cool for a few minutes, then cut them apart. Serve warm or allow to coo , and refrigerate in sealed containers. Reheat before serving.

COOK'S NOTES
• Baking sausage rolls as one large roll before cutting through makes them neater and prevents the filling from shrinking and drying while baking.
• Sausage rolls freeze very well, raw or cooked. Allow to thaw and bake or reheat before serving.
• Adjust the size according to preference for smaller or larger sausage rolls.

CHEESE TARTLETS

Makes 12 tartlets

SAVOURY TARTLET PASTRY

240 g (500 ml) Golden Cloud cake flour
15 ml baking powder
2 ml salt
250 g (280 ml) butter or hard
  margarine, cut into cubes
  and softened
30 ml white vinegar
2 eggs
additional flour for kneading and rolling

CHEESE FILLING

30 ml butter or hard margarine
50 ml cake flour
250 ml milk
1 egg
100 g (250 ml) grated cheddar cheese
salt and milled black pepper
Red Sprinkle Mix (page 12)

1 Preheat the oven to 180°C. Generously grease 12 cups of a standard muffin tin.
2 To make the pastry, place all the ingredients into a mixing bowl, or the bowl of a food processor. Mix or process just until the dough holds together. Or, rub the butter or margarine into the dry ingredients. Beat together the vinegar and eggs, add to the pastry, and mix just until the dough holds together.
3 Turn the pastry out onto a floured surface. If it's too soft, add a little extra flour. Knead lightly until smooth. Press into a ball, cover and refrigerate while preparing the filling.
4 To make the filling, melt the butter or margarine in a medium saucepan. Remove from the heat and blend in the flour and milk. Bring to the boil, stirring constantly, until smooth and thick.
5 Beat the egg in a bowl. Beat in a little of the hot sauce, and pour it back into the saucepan.

Stir in the cheese until melted, and season with salt and pepper. Set aside to cool.
6 Roll out the pastry, on a floured surface, with a lightly floured rolling pin until quite thin (5 mm). Cut out with an 8 cm round cutter. Place the pastry over the muffin cups and press down neatly, using a little ball of dough to do so to prevent piercing with your fingernails. Freeze the leftover pastry.
7 Divide the filling between the lined cups, sprinkle with the seasoning and bake for about 20 minutes, until the pastry is golden, and the filling is puffed and firm. Serve hot, warm, or at room temperature.

COOK'S NOTES
- Uncooked pastry circles can be separated with clingfilm, sealed and frozen.
- Refrigerate baked tartlets for up to 2 days, and reheat at 160° C for 8–10 minutes.

CHEESE TARTLET VARIATIONS

Tuna Tartlets
Reduce the filling cheese by half, and add a 200 g tin of tuna, drained and flaked, and 30 ml chopped fresh parsley.

Asparagus Tartlets
Reduce the filling cheese by half, and add 200 g of tinned asparagus salad cuts, well drained, and 30 ml chopped fresh parsley.

Spinach and Feta Tartlets
Omit the filling cheese and add 200 ml lightly cooked, drained, chopped spinach, 125 ml finely diced or crumbled feta cheese, and 30 ml chopped spring onion. Season with grated nutmeg and dried dill.

Mixed Vegetable Tartlets
Omit the cheese in the filling and add 250 ml mixed chopped, cooked vegetables, and 30 ml chopped fresh parsley.

Mushroom and Cheese Tartlets
Lightly fry 250 g sliced mushrooms and 50 ml chopped onion in a little oil until tender. Add 1 ml dried oregano and 15 ml white wine; simmer until the liquid has evaporated. Stir into the cheese filling.

CURRIED FISH TARTLETS

Makes 24–30 tartlets, depending on size

CREAM CHEESE PASTRY
250 g (280 ml) butter or hard
    margarine, cubed and softened
250 g (250 ml) creamed cottage cheese
240 g (500 ml) Golden Cloud cake flour
CURRIED FISH FILLING
2 x 105–120 g tins sardines or smoked
    oysters, drained, or 150–200 g
    smoked mackerel, flaked
7 ml mild curry powder
2 ml hot curry powder (optional)
30 ml mayonnaise
2 hard-boiled eggs, peeled and mashed
15 ml finely chopped fresh parsley
GLAZE
1 egg
15 ml milk

1 Place the butter or margarine, cottage cheese and flour into a bowl. Mix with a fork until the pastry holds together.
2 Turn out onto a floured surface and knead lightly to form a smooth, soft dough. Cover, and refrigerate for at least 1 hour.
3 To make the filling, mash together all the ingredients with a fork until well blended.
4 Preheat the oven to 200°C. Grease two medium baking trays. Roll out the pastry with a floured rolling pin onto a floured surface. Lift the pastry as necessary, and sprinkle more flour on the work surface. Roll out to a thickness of about 5 mm.
5 Cut the pastry into 8–10 cm circles, making them as close together as possible to prevent having to reroll the pastry too often. Reroll the offcuts and cut into circles.
6 Spoon the filling in the centre of the circles. Carefully and neatly fold the dough over the filling, and press gently to seal the edge. Mark lightly with a fork.
7 Beat together the egg and milk for the glaze, and brush onto the pies. Place onto the trays, slightly apart, and bake for 12–15 minutes, until golden. Serve warm or cold.

COOK'S NOTES
• Cream cheese pastry is one of the simplest pastries to prepare, and is delicious and crisp – perfect for small savouries or snacks.
• The pastry and filling can be chilled overnight. Leave it at room temperature for a while, so that it's easy to roll out.
• Roll out leftover pastry to 60–80 mm, and cut into decorative shapes; top with grated cheese and Red Sprinkle Mix (page 12). Bake with the pies until golden and crisp.
• These pies can be frozen after shaping or baking. Thaw and bake or reheat when required.

CURRIED FISH TARTLET VARIATIONS

Curried Chicken Tartlets
Replace the fish in the filling with 200 g (250 ml) chopped, cooked chicken and 15 ml finely chopped onion.
Curried Cheese Tartlets
Replace the fish in the filling with the following ingredients mixed together: 200 g (500 ml) grated cheddar or emmental, 50 g (125 ml) soft cheese (ricotta, firm cream cheese or feta), 1 egg, 1 ml dry English mustard, and 1 ml garlic and herb seasoning. Sprinkle the tartlets with Red Sprinkle Mix (page 12), coarse salt, or sesame or poppy seeds.

SAVOURY PUFF PASTRY STACK

Makes 6–8 large stacks, or 10–12 small stacks

Layers of crisp puff pastry filled with a creamy savoury filling. This recipe requires little effort to prepare, but the results are fantastic. Makes an impressive starter or light meal with a vegetable or salad garnish.

PUFF PASTRY

250 g (280 ml) butter or hard margarine (ice cold)

240 g (500 ml) Golden Cloud cake flour

1 ml salt

1 egg yolk

15 ml white vinegar

125 ml ice-cold water

additional cake flour for rolling

CREAM FILLING

50 g (50 ml) butter or hard margarine, chilled

60 g (125 ml) Golden Cloud cake flour

500 ml milk

125 ml cream or sour cream

salt and milled black pepper

30 ml finely chopped spring onion, leek or onion

additional filling ingredients (see Variations)

50 g (125 ml) finely grated cheddar cheese, or similar tasty cheese for sprinkling

1 To make the pastry: grate the butter or margarine on a coarse grater and place in the freezer for at least 30 minutes – several hours is even better.

2 Place the flour, frozen grated butter or margarine, and salt into a large bowl. Mix evenly with a fork. Make a well in the centre.

3 Beat together the egg yolks, vinegar and water, and add to the flour. Mix with a fork until the pastry starts to hold together, but is still quite crumbly; it will gradually form into dough while rolling and folding. Press into a ball and place on a lightly floured surface.

COOK'S NOTES

- This puff pastry recipe is simple, quick and versatile, and makes about 500 g of pastry.
- If you're not planning to serve the dish within an hour or two, refrigerate the completed stack before baking. Allow a little extra warming time. Alternatively, keep the baked pastry and filling separate until just before serving, then reheat the filling, assemble the stack and heat as described.

SAVOURY PUFF PASTRY STACK VARIATIONS

Puff Pastry Chicken Stack
Add to the filling 400 g cooked, shredded or diced chicken, mixed with 200 g sliced button mushrooms, lightly fried in oil, or a 400 g tin asparagus salad cuts, drained. Season with or dried mixed herbs.

Puff Pastry Seafood Stack
Add to the filling 2 x 200 g tins drained, flaked tuna or salmon, or cooked fish, poached haddock or seafood mix, thawed, drained, and cooked, and 3 hard-boiled eggs, coarsely chopped. If you wish, add 5–10 ml chopped capers and 30 ml chopped fresh parsley. Flavour with a little lemon juice or a few drops of Tabasco sauce, tomato sauce, and garlic and herb seasoning.

4 Sprinkle the crumbly pastry with flour, and roll out with a floured rolling pin to an oblong approximately 20 mm thick. Fold the short edges to meet in the centre and close like a book.

5 Turn the pastry at 90°, sprinkle lightly with more flour, and fold again as before. Repeat 4 to 5 times, until the pastry is smooth, sprinkling with extra flour as and when necessary. Don't roll and fold more than 6 times; the pastry will be less flaky. Cover and refrigerate the dough for at least 1 hour (preferably overnight).

6 Preheat the oven to 220°C. Roll out the pastry on a floured surface to a thickness of about 4 mm. Lift and shake the pastry to allow for shrinkage, and cut into 2–3 even strips, about 30 x 15 cm each, or into 2–3 x 26 cm circles, depending on how many layers are needed. Press the remaining pastry together and refrigerate or freeze for later use.

7 Place the pastry on ungreased baking trays, and bake for about 15 minutes until well puffed, golden and crisp. Don't overbake – the pastry is delicate and the texture and flavour will be spoilt. Allow to cool on a wire rack while preparing the filling. Meanwhile, reduce the oven temperature to 160°C.

8 To make the filling, melt the butter or margarine in a medium saucepan. Remove from the heat and blend in the flour and milk. Bring to the boil, stirring until smooth and thick. Remove from the heat, and stir in the cream or sour cream; season with salt and pepper. Reserve one-third of the sauce.

9 Stir the spring onion, leek or onion into the remaining sauce with the additional ingredients of your choice. Stack layers of puff pastry and filling onto a baking tray. Spread the reserved sauce on top, and sprinkle with cheese.

10 Heat the pastry stack through for about 8–10 minutes. Cut into squares or wedges.

CHEESE AND ONION QUICHE

Makes 1 large pie

A simple, easy-to-make savoury pie, with crisp yet tender and moist pastry.

SAVOURY BUTTERMILK PASTRY
120 g (250 ml) Golden Cloud cake flour
7 ml baking powder
1 ml salt
50 ml sunflower oil
75 ml buttermilk, plus a little extra
   if necessary
CHEESE AND ONION FILLING
1 large onion, roughly chopped
50 g (50 ml) butter or hard margarine
60 g (125 ml) Golden Cloud cake flour
750 ml milk
salt and white pepper
30 ml chopped spring onion
30 ml chopped fresh parsley
150 g (375 ml) grated cheddar cheese
3 eggs
meat, fish or vegetable filling
   (see Variations)
GARNISH
chopped fresh parsley
freshly milled black pepper or ground
   paprika (optional)

1 Generously grease a 25 cm deep or 28 cm shallow pie dish.
2 Place the ingredients for the pastry into a mixing bowl (to mix by hand), or the bowl of an electric mixer fitted with the dough hook. Mix gently to form a dough. Add a little extra buttermilk if it's too stiff. Don't overmix, as this will toughen the pastry.
3 Press the pastry evenly into the base and sides of the pie dish, making it thinner in the corners. Trim the edges, crimping with your fingers, or cut away with a sharp knife. Blend the offcuts into the base. Refrigerate while making the filling. Preheat the oven to 180°C.
4 Fry the onion in the butter or margarine in a medium saucepan, until translucent. Remove from the heat and stir in the flour and milk; season with salt and pepper. Cook over moderate heat, stirring constantly, until smooth and thick. Remove from the heat and stir in spring onion, parsley and cheese.
5 Beat the eggs in a large bowl. Stir in the cooked filling, and allow to cool.
6 Stir in the meat, fish or vegetable ingredients of your choice. Spoon the filling into the pastry-lined dish. Sprinkle lightly with parsley and dust with pepper or paprika, if using. Bake for about 40 minutes, until the pie is set and light golden.
7 Serve warm with salad and fresh bread.

COOK'S NOTES
- For a light, fluffy pie, separate the eggs, add the yolks to the sauce and, in a separate bowl, whip the whites until stiff, then fold into the sauce. You will need a slightly deeper or larger pie dish if you prepare the pie in this manner.
- For a firmer pie to cut into slices or portions, add an extra egg to the filling

CHEESE AND ONION QUICHE VARIATIONS

Add 2 of any of the fillings listed below, mixed and matched as you please.

200 g bacon, cooked and chopped
200 g ham, diced or cut into strips
200 g cooked chicken, diced or shredded
200 g tin tuna, drained and flaked
2 x 185 g tins salmon, drained and flaked
200 g button mushrooms, sliced and fried
200 g drained, tinned asparagus salad cuts
200 g chopped, cooked and drained spinach
200 g cooked broccoli florets, well drained

MEDITERRANEAN PHYLLO PIE

Makes 1 large pie

A great-looking pie to serve as a light meal or side dish to a meat main course, or at a braai.

olive oil for brushing and frying
300 g spinach, washed, drained and
  coarsely chopped
250 ml sliced leeks
1 clove garlic, peeled and crushed
50 g (50 ml) butter or hard margarine
50 ml Golden Cloud cake flour
300 ml milk
15 ml dijon or wholegrain mustard
5 ml mixed dried herbs
125 g ricotta cheese or chunky
  cottage cheese
2 eggs
250 ml finely chopped cooked chicken
  or ham
salt or milled black pepper

PHYLLO PASTRY CRUST

8 sheets ready-made phyllo pastry
30 ml olive oil, or melted butter or
  margarine for brushing

1 Preheat the oven to180°C. Brush a 24 cm springform tin with olive oil.
2 Heat a little olive oil in a medium frying pan. Stir-fry the spinach, leeks and garlic in the oil, until the vegetables are limp, and most of the liquid has evaporated.
3 Melt the butter or margarine in a medium saucepan. Remove from the heat and whisk in the flour and milk. Cook over moderate heat, stirring constantly, until smooth and thickened. Remove from the heat and add the mustard, herbs, the cooked vegetable mixture, cheese, eggs and chicken or ham. Season with salt and pepper. Cover and set aside to cool.
4 Layer six sheets of phyllo pastry on a worktop to form a star, brushing each layer with oil or melted butter or margarine. Place into the prepared tin, pressing into the corners. Spoon in the filling and cover with the remaining sheets of pastry, brushing each layer as before. Fold in bit by bit to cover the filling, and press down neatly.
5 Bake for about 40 minutes, until the tart is set and slightly risen in the centre, and the filling is hot. Turn out, then turn over onto a serving platter. Cut into wedges and serve hot.

COOK'S NOTES

• This pie can also be made with Savoury Buttermilk Pastry (page 118). Line a 25 cm deep or 28 cm shallow pie dish with the pastry and fill as described above.
• For a vegetarian pie, omit the chicken and ham, or replace it with lightly cooked vegetables such as courgettes, cabbage and green or red peppers.

POTATO, LEEK AND CHEESE PIE

Makes 1 large pie

Perfect for brunch, a light lunch or supper.

Savoury Buttermilk Pastry (page 118)
300 g potatoes (3 medium potatoes)
salt and white pepper
250 ml finely sliced young leeks
30 g (30 ml) butter or hard margarine
100 g (250 ml) grated cheddar cheese
3 eggs
125 ml milk
125 ml cream or additional milk
1 ml garlic and herb seasoning
milled black pepper

1 Generously grease a deep 25 cm or a shallow 28 cm pie dish. Prepare the pastry and line the dish with it.

2 Place the potatoes into a medium saucepan, cover with water and simmer for about 15 minutes, until just tender if pierced with a skewer. Drain and rinse with cold water. Peel and slice thinly (approximately 5 mm). Season with salt.

3 Fry the leeks in butter or margarine in a medium saucepan, until translucent, stirring from time to time. Salt lightly and allow to cool. Preheat the oven to 180°C.

4 Spread the leeks evenly onto the crust. Arrange potato slices on top, overlapping neatly. Sprinkle the cheese on top.

5 Beat together the eggs, milk and cream, and season with salt, white pepper, and garlic and herb seasoning. Pour onto the potato and cheese, and dust with black pepper. Bake for about 35 minutes, until the filling has set and the top is golden brown.

COOK'S NOTE
Add about 100 g chopped cooked bacon, or ham for a meaty pie.

CHICKEN AND BROCCOLI PIE

Makes 1 large pie

A wholesome, homely pie, excellent for coffee shops and home industries.

CHICKEN AND BROCCOLI FILLING
200 g chicken breast fillets
100 ml chicken stock
200 g broccoli florets
50 g (125 ml) finely grated tasty cheese
   (cheddar or edam)
200 ml hot milk
250 ml cream (or half cream, half milk)
6 eggs
10 ml mayonnaise
1 ml curry powder
30–50 ml chopped spring onion
salt and milled black pepper
2 ml mixed dried herbs
pinch grated nutmeg
Red Sprinkle Mix (page 12), or paprika

QUICK SAVOURY CRUST
120 g (250 ml) Golden Cloud cake flour,
   or 140 g (250 ml) Golden Cloud
   Krakley Wheat wholewheat flour
   (or use half and half)
1 ml salt
2 ml baking powder
80 g (80 ml) butter or hard margarine,
   softened
1 egg
few drops of water if necessary

COOK'S NOTES
• It's important to heat the milk so that the filling is not too cold at the start of baking. This will prolong the time needed for the pie to set in the centre.
• For individual tartlets, line 12 small tartlet pans with pastry and prepare as described above. Bake about 20 minutes, or until the crust is cooked and the filling has set.
• For a low-fat pie, use milk only, or low-fat evaporated milk.

1 Preheat the oven to 180°C. Grease a 25 cm deep or 28 cm shallow pie dish.
2 Place the chicken fillets into a saucepan. Add the stock, cover and simmer for 15 minutes, or until cooked. Or, cook in a covered microwave-safe container in the microwave on Medium for 4–5 minutes. Allow to cool.
3 Rinse the broccoli, and boil in a saucepan with water for 8–10 minutes, until tender. Drain and set aside to cool.
4 Place all the ingredients for the crust into a mixing bowl or the bowl of a food processor, and mix or process, adding a little water if necessary, until evenly combined into a soft pastry. Or mix and knead by hand to a soft dough.
5 Press the pastry evenly into the pie plate, thinning it out in the corners and crimping it with your fingers to make a neat edge.

Scatter half of the cheese onto the base, and refrigerate.
6 Mix together the hot milk and cream. Add the eggs, mayonnaise, curry powder and spring onion, and season with herbs, nutmeg, salt and pepper, and beat well until evenly combined. Set aside.
7 Cut the cooled chicken and broccoli into chunks and scatter over the cheese in the crust. Pour in the egg mixture to fill the dish to no more than 5 mm below the edge. If there's a little left over, add to another sauce or egg dish.
8 Sprinkle the remaining cheese and the Red Sprinkle Mix on top, and bake for about 40 minutes, until pale golden and firm, and set in the centre. Serve warm, or cool and then cover and refrigerate until required. Reheat at 180°C for 10–15 minutes.

FETA PIE

Makes 1 pie

Simple but oh so good! Serve warm or at room temperature with a Greek-style salad made with olives, tomatoes and spring onion.

Savoury Buttermilk Pastry (page 118)
4 eggs
250 g feta cheese, plain, or flavoured
    with herbs and black pepper
250 ml cream
100 ml milk
salt and white pepper (optional)
sprigs of fresh parsley to garnish

COOK'S NOTE

To serve as a centrepiece for a salad, use a 22 cm tart pan with a removable fluted rim, or a 22 cm loose-bottomed cake tin. Remove the pie from the tin when cool.

FETA PIE VARIATIONS

Add 250 ml cooked, cooled and well-drained chopped spinach or grated beetroot. Other interesting options are 50 ml sun-dried tomatoes in oil, or peppadews, drained and coarsely chopped, chopped anchovies, or chopped stoned olives. Scatter onto the pastry before pouring over the filling.

1 Preheat the oven to 180°C. Grease a 22 cm pie dish or a tin with a removable rim (see Cook's note).

2 Prepare the pastry, and line the pie dish as described in step 3 for Cheese and Onion Quiche (page 118).

3 Separate the eggs. Place the yolks, feta, cream and milk into a food processor. Process until smooth. Whip egg white until stiff. Fold into the feta mixture, and season lightly with salt and pepper (if using), taking into account the saltiness of the cheese.

4 Pour into the prepared pie dish or tin, and bake for about 30 minutes, until set. Allow to cool to room temperature before serving.

HERBED TUNA AND TOMATO PIE

Makes 1 large pie

Quick Savoury Crust (page 121), or
    Savoury Buttermilk Pastry (page 118)
350 g ripe red tomatoes
    or a 410 g tin whole peeled tomatoes
1 medium onion, finely chopped
1 clove garlic, peeled and crushed
30 ml sunflower or olive oil
5 ml dried oregano
200 g tin tuna, drained and flaked
40 g (100 ml) grated cheddar cheese
3 eggs
250 ml cream
salt and milled black pepper
8–10 black or calamata olives (optional)
50 g anchovy fillets (optional)

1 Preheat the oven to 180°C. Prepare the pastry and line a deep 25 cm or a shallow 28 cm pie dish.
2 If using fresh tomatoes, place them into a bowl and pour over boiling water to cover. Set aside for a few minutes, then remove and peel and chop coarsely. If using tinned tomatoes, chop them in their liquid.
3 Fry the onion and garlic in oil until translucent, stirring from time to time. Add the tomato and oregano and simmer until most of the moisture has evaporated. Stir in the tuna, and allow to cool.
4 Sprinkle half of the cheese onto the crust. Cover with the filling, and sprinkle with the remaining cheese. Beat together the eggs and cream; season with salt and pepper, and pour onto the filling. Arrange stoned olives and anchovy fillets (if using) on top.
5 Bake for about 30 minutes until the crust is golden and crisp, and the filling has set. Serve warm with a green salad for lunch or a light dinner.

HERBED TUNA AND TOMATO PIE VARIATION

Substitute tinned salmon, smoked trout or mackerel, or seafood mix (thawed, drained and cooked) for the tuna.
Combine different types of cheese such as mozzarella, edam or feta, according to preference and availability.

HOME-MADE PIZZA

Makes 2 large or 3 medium pizzas

PIZZA DOUGH

10 g sachet instant yeast
240 g (500 ml) Golden Cloud cake flour,
    or 280 g (500 ml) Golden Cloud
    white bread flour
10 ml sugar
7 ml salt
250 ml lukewarm water
30 ml sunflower or olive oil
120 g (250 ml) extra Golden Cloud cake
    flour or 140 g (250 ml) extra Golden
    Cloud white bread flour (approximate
    amount)

TOMATO BASE

400 g very ripe tomatoes, or
    410 g tin tomato and onion mix
30 ml chopped fresh herbs, 10 ml mixed
    dried herbs
1–2 cloves garlic, peeled and crushed,
    or 5 ml garlic and herb seasoning
sugar, salt and milled black pepper

OPTIONAL TOPPING INGREDIENTS

a mix of any or all of the following
    ingredients:
stoned olives (any type)
strips of red or green peppers
sliced mushrooms
snipped spring onions
slivers of green or red chillies
sun-dried tomatoes
peppadews

CHEESE TOPPING

200 g (500 ml) cheese, grated, sliced or
    crumbled (see Cheese Toppings)

1 Place the yeast and the first measure of flour
  into a mixing bowl, or the bowl of an electric
  mixer fitted with the dough hook. Mix to
  combine. Add all the remaining ingredients
  – except the extra flour – and mix well.
2 Add enough extra flour to form a soft
  dough. Knead for 4-5 minutes (in the mixer)
  or turn out onto a floured surface and knead
  by hand for 5-6 minutes, until smooth and
  elastic. Shape the dough into a ball and
  return it to the bowl. Cover and allow to rise
  for about 30 minutes, until doubled in bulk.
3 To make the tomato base, prepare the fresh
  tomatoes by placing it into a bowl, and
  covering with boiling water. Set aside for
  a few minutes; drain, skin and slice. Drain in
  a colander for at least 30 minutes. Place the
  tomatoes or tin of tomato and onion mix
  into a bowl. Flavour with herbs garlic, sugar,
  salt and pepper.
4 Preheat the oven to 180°C. Grease 2 large
  (30 cm) pizza plates or 3 shallow (24 cm) pie
  dishes. Divide the dough in half or into 3,
  and press evenly into the dishes, making it
  6–10 cm thick. It will rise to double the
  thickness while baking.
5 Spread an even layer of tomato base onto
  the dough. Watchpoint: if you have used
  fresh tomato, sprinkle a thin layer of the
  cheese onto the dough first, and arrange
  the tomatoes on top to prevent the dough
  from becoming soggy.
6 Arrange selected optional ingredients on
  top, and sprinkle with the cheese topping.
  Bake for 20–25 minutes, until the crust is
  firm and golden, and the topping is sizzling.

CHEESE TOPPINGS

Mozzarella melts to a creamy yet
slightly stringy topping.
It is great with salty ingredients such
as anchovies, bacon, salami and olives.
Parmesan and pecorino should be finely
grated or shaved.
Rabiola, a firm, tasty goat milk cheese
adds a distinct flavour.
Cheddar is firm and tasty; a good
stand-in for any other cheese.
Goat milk cheese and roughly crumbled
feta are an interesting addition
to pizzas.
Fontina, gruyère, gorgonzola, emmental
and edam add exciting flavours.
For a Four Cheese Pizza, use mozzarella
plus three other cheeses of your choice.

PIZZA VARIATIONS

Pizza Margherita
Tomato base, mozzarella, chopped fresh
basil leaves or dried basil,
grated parmesan.

Pizza Napolitana
Tomato base, mozzarella, drained
anchovies, additional fresh or dried
oregano, and stoned olives.

Pizza Romano
Thinly sliced onion rings, drained,
tinned red pimentos, peppadews, or
sliced peppers, anchovy fillets.

Pizza con Pollo
Spicy strips of cooked chicken breasts
and/or chicken livers (use Cajun or
Mexican seasoning), onion rings, garlic
and/or mushrooms and asparagus.

Pizza Hawaiian
Fresh or drained, tinned pineapple
chunks, diced or shredded ham, and
finely sliced or chopped mixed peppers.

Pizza Marinara
Seafood such as cooked marinara mix
or drained, tinned tuna or salmon
and/or blanched calamari rings,
chopped capers, finely chopped
peppers, asparagus or mushrooms.

Biltong and Avocado Pizza
Tomato base, thinly sliced avocado and
a combination of cheeses.

Bacon / Ham / Salami Pizza
Tomato base, mozzarella, cooked,
crumbled rindless bacon, ham or
salami, sliced mushrooms, drained,
tinned asparagus or cooked, sliced
courgettes or pattypans. For a more
colourful pizza, add finely sliced
peppers, and stoned olives.

Pizza Bolognaise
Spread cooled bolognaise sauce onto
the base instead of the tomato.
Top with mozzarella.

Pizza Moussaka
Fried aubergine slices, bolognaise sauce
and grated cheese.

Vegetarian Pizza
Tomato base, lightly cooked young
vegetables (courgettes, pattypans,
aubergines) and drained, sliced, tinned
artichokes; sliced raw mushrooms,
onion rings and drained, tinned
asparagus; chopped sun-dried tomatoes
and crumbled goat milk cheese.

INDEX